# Exploding
# the Truth

## The JFK, Jr., Assassination

# Exploding
# the Truth

## The JFK, Jr., Assassination

John Koerner

Winchester, UK
Washington, USA

First published by Chronos Books, 2018
Chronos Books is an imprint of John Hunt Publishing Ltd., No. 3 East St., Alresford,
Hampshire SO24 9EE, UK
office1@jhpbooks.net
www.johnhuntpublishing.com

For distributor details and how to order please visit the 'Ordering' section on our website.

Text copyright: John Koerner 2017

ISBN: 978 1 78535 884 5
978 1 78535 885 2 (ebook)
Library of Congress Control Number: 2017956155

A CIP catalogue record for this book is available from the British Library.

Design: Stuart Davies

Printed and bound by CPI Group (UK) Ltd, Croydon, CR0 4YY, UK

We operate a distinctive and ethical publishing philosophy in
all areas of our business, from our global network of authors to
production and worldwide distribution.

# Contents

For Amanda

# Introduction

When trying to prove the existence of a conspiracy it is essential to systematically dismantle the lies that filter into the accepted versions of historical events. The death of John F. Kennedy, Jr., was nothing more than a tragic accident. That is what nearly two decades of misinformation has led many people to believe. It will be the purpose of this book to logically dispel that notion, and prove beyond any reasonable doubt that the events of July 16, 1999, were instead a skillfully planned assassination. It was covered up by powerful forces intent on silencing him for political, personal, and historical reasons that reach back to his father's administration in the 1960s.

The death of John F. Kennedy, Jr., was one of the most tragic days in the 20th Century. Here was a man who seemed to have everything, but was cut down in his prime. He was the publisher of a successful magazine, *George*, the husband to a beautiful wife, Caroline, and the heir to the Kennedy throne if he ever chose to run for office. As we will explore, towards the end of his life he increasingly felt the need to get more involved in politics, especially through his magazine, as confirmed by private discussions with his friends about continuing the Kennedy tradition of public service. He also became aware of the dark forces behind his father's assassination, and felt obligated to quietly pursue the truth. Was this making him a threat?

On a personal note, I hope and pray that this will not be my last book, for two reasons. First, I have written conspiracy books about JFK, President William McKinley, and investigations of Christian mystics. None of these books have enjoyed the level of national impact that I had hoped they would achieve. Each one rewrote basic tenants of accepted, mainstream historical facts, with nothing but logic and evidence. One grows tired of trying to change the world when so few people are willing to listen.

Second, the only book that has seen some level of national media exposure was my book about the Kennedy assassination, titled *Why the C.I.A. Killed JFK and Malcolm X: The Secret Drug Trade in Laos.* but even that fell short of my lofty expectations. However, it did not seem to go unnoticed at least in some private quarters. What I am about to share can be verified by any number of doctors and nurses who saved my life in the summer of 2014 at Buffalo General Hospital. I was about to sign the final contract to send my book to the printer when I became gravely ill. I pride myself on maintaining a healthy lifestyle. I do not smoke, drink alcohol, or do any recreational drugs. I also exercise regularly, so it was surprising to me that I became so instantaneously sick. My face, lungs, and heart filled with fluid, as my muscles atrophied. I dropped nearly 40 pounds in a matter of days. At one point my family was told that there was nothing more that could be done for me. I am very grateful that I am alive today, and still can be a father to my two beautiful children. I was asked several times by different doctors if I had ever traveled to Southeast Asia. I do not even have a passport. Apparently, whatever disease I got had never once appeared anywhere that they could find in the United States, only rarely in Southeast Asia, and even that was only a guess. During the research for my JFK book, I learned about the death of journalist Gary Webb of the *San Jose Mercury News* who was likely killed by the C.I.A. Like me, he was also involved in exposing how the agency was involved in the drug running business. It scared me even further when I found out later that year in 2014 a movie was released titled, *Kill the Messenger*, that chronicled Webb's effort to expose the truth. I do not want to be the next one to be silenced. I am aware that no one else has ever written a mainstream book about the possibility that JFK, Jr., was the victim of an assassination conspiracy, perhaps for good reason. If that is the case, the conspirators are likely still alive. In the spirit of President Kennedy's call to service in his inauguration address, I am willing to do my part to serve my country in the way that I know best, to expose the truth. This is what I can do for my country, like my grandfather did fighting the Nazis in World War II, or my father as part of NATO forces defending Europe during the Cold War. My family has served proudly in every branch of the military. Semper Fidelis – to the truth.

John Koerner
August 2017

# Part I

# The Motives

## Chapter One

# Exonerating the Clintons

Trying to figure out who was behind the assassination of John F. Kennedy, Jr., is nearly as complicated and controversial as untangling the dark web of forces behind his father's slaying. In looking at the evidence though, there appears to be two primary lines of thinking that could lead us to logically conclude that some powerful people wanted this man dead.

The first area we will explore is John F. Kennedy, Jr.'s, desire to enter the world of politics, something he had shunned his whole life. If this was true, it would put him in the way of some potentially dangerous people who had their own designs on obtaining the reins of power.

Second, it appears likely that at the end of his life, JFK, Jr., was becoming increasingly aware that the C.I.A. organized the assassination of his father. This fact may have been why he became a publisher, to have a platform to expose the truth to the world, and bring to justice those still alive who planned his father's execution.

Let us first explore the possibility that John F. Kennedy, Jr., was seriously considering running for governor of New York, and eventually president. This, according to his closest friends, was exactly what was on his mind in the last months of his life. His assistant at *George*, Rose Marie Terenzio, told *People* in a July 2016 cover story that he was planning on running for president. After Republican New York Senator Alphonse D'Amato told Kennedy he should run for mayor of New York City, he apparently laughed it off. After this encounter with D'Amato, Terenzio asked why he would not want to consider it. His answer pointed to a much loftier goal, a shrewd political calculation that would have made his father proud.

"Well, Rosie, how many mayors do you know that become President?" Kennedy said to Terenzio. "I was so shocked I didn't say anything. Then he smirked as if to say 'That's not the road you go down. We'll see what happens.'"

The mayor of a city is not a large enough platform to stage a run for the White House, no matter who you are. However, the U.S. Senate, or being the governor of a prominent state like New York could have been just the stepping stone that he had in mind to launch his presidential bid, likely in 2004. In fact, several of his friends knew he was seriously considering running for governor. The next election for governor would have been in 2002. He would have faced George Pataki, who at that time was seeking a third term. Most people voting that year did not vote for Pataki, as he garnered an unimpressive 49% of the popular vote. He largely ran on his record of leadership during the September 11, 2001, terrorist attacks in New York City. The one candidate who could have counteracted this appeal would have been JFK, Jr., a longtime resident of New York City. Kennedy probably would have personally known many of the people who died in the attack, and likely would have aided in the recovery. There is no doubt that his potential appeal as a candidate no matter what office he ran for would have energized New York State Democrats like no one else. A fellow Democrat from New York, Mark Green, mulling over his own run for the Senate, conducted a private poll in 1997 to see who Democrats liked the most within their state. "He was by far the most popular Democrat," Green said. "He had the highest favorable-unfavorable spread; 65% of Democrats rated him favorably and 10% rated him unfavorably." Former New York State Democratic Chairman John Marino said that if Kennedy ever ran for office, "it would have been, goodbye, anyone else." Such a campaign would have been much like when his uncle Robert Kennedy won his New York U. S. Senate seat by an impressive 10-point margin, 53% to 43%, over incumbent Republican Kenneth Keating in 1964. Assuming Kennedy won the election in November 2002, he would have become New York's 54th governor on January 1, 2003.

Would a short time in Albany be enough to run for president in 2004, to prevent George W. Bush from getting a second term? Many of our presidents at one time were governor of New York, often for very shorts stints. Martin Van Buren, our nation's 8th president, was only governor for 3 months from January 1, 1829, to March 5, 1829. Grover Cleveland, the 22nd and the 24th president, was only governor for one year when he announced his candidacy for president in 1884. Theodore Roosevelt spent only one year as governor as well before agreeing to run with William McKinley as his vice-presidential nominee in the election of 1900, after which he ascended to the presidency a few months later following McKinley's assassination in September 1901. Franklin Roosevelt was in the middle of what would be his only term as governor when he began his campaign for president in the early 1930s. We could even mention Democrat Samuel J. Tilden, the 25th governor of New York, who spent only one year as governor before accepting the nomination of his party in the summer of 1876. Most historians agree the presidency was stolen from him later that year in a corrupt deal worked out in the Congress that gave the presidency to the Republicans, otherwise he would have become the nation's 19th president.

Also in that *People* article was the testimony of Gary Ginsberg, a friend from their time together at Brown University, as well as a business partner who helped Kennedy start *George* magazine. Ginsberg was with Kennedy the night before he died and had this to say about his mindset. "By July 1999, I think he could take great comfort that he had started and led a successful business, had fulfilled his mission to cover politics in a colorful, non-ideological way that would make it appealing for people who had never bought a political magazine before, and was now in a position to do something new." According to Ginsberg the New York Senate seat was also on his mind but eventually decided against that path, out of deference to first lady Hillary Clinton, a friend and fellow Democrat. "He had been thinking about running for the N.Y. Senate seat. He even had meetings about it that spring, but by July had concluded he would focus his attention on running for governor of N.Y." The next election for governor was 2002. His longtime friend felt this was a better fit for him anyway. This is an important point we need to make here. Kennedy had decided against running for the Senate. Many have laid the blame at the feet of the Clintons for this assassination. The fact that he was making it clear he had no intention of running against Clinton is no small point. "By temperament and interest, John, I think, realized he was far more suited to being a governor than a legislator. He knew from running *George* that he could be an inspiring, strong chief executive of a state, setting the tone for government and successfully running a complex operation," said Ginsberg.

We need to establish clearly that Kennedy posed no political threat to Hillary Clinton in 1999 because he had decided not to run against her for the Senate nomination. This removes the only motives the Clintons would have had to conspire to kill him. It was clear that Kennedy had no intention of joining the race if it meant going head to head against the Clintons. There was a mutual respect and admiration that existed between both families that dated back to a fateful encounter during the Kennedy presidency. On July 24, 1963, 16-year-old Bill Clinton shook hands with JFK at the White House Rose Garden. Clinton was in Washington to attend activities sponsored by the American Legion Boys Nation program. The future president said it was that handshake that inspired him to want to enter a life of public service. Clinton was part of a group of 100 teenage boys representing their home states as they spent a week in the capital visiting with Secretary of State Dean Rusk, debating issues, passing mock legislation, and staging elections. This event meant so much to Clinton that just six months into his own presidency, Clinton staged a reunion at the White House in July 1993 to mark the 30-year anniversary of the famous handshake. About 70 "alumni" and their families showed up to have breakfast with the president, and make a pilgrimage to Arlington National Cemetery to visit John F. Kennedy's Eternal Flame gravesite. This no doubt brought back some difficult memories of the assassination for President Clinton who said he was "heartbroken" when he heard the news. His reflections were part of an NBC special report on November 22, 2013, titled "Where Were You?" Clinton recounted a special bond he and Hillary Clinton shared with Jackie Kennedy, and how she was a key early supporter of his run for the presidency.

"Later in her life, after I became president and even when I was running, Hillary and I became friends with her. For reasons I never fully understood, she supported me in the primary in 1992, and she came to one of my early events in New York. One of my prized pictures is sitting with her at dinner in the summertime in Martha's Vineyard. I just loved her, and Hillary really was close to her." Clinton, like so many of his generation, respected and idealized the Kennedy family. "In a way they symbolized our growing up, our aspirations. For my whole generation, the first time we looked at politics, there they were, and we liked what we saw. In her case, because I really got to know her, the more I knew her, the more I liked her."

It is also important to note that in his first year in office, President Clinton appointed JFK's sister Jean Ann Kennedy Smith to serve as United States Ambassador to Ireland. She was quickly confirmed by the Senate, and stayed at that post for his entire first term. The connection between the families extended even beyond death. After JFK, Jr.'s, plane crash, a private funeral mass was held for Kennedy and his wife, on July 23, 1999, at the Church of St. Thomas More in Manhattan. This was where Jacqueline Kennedy Onassis had worshipped. Among the 300 invited guests for this closed ceremony were President Bill

Clinton and Hillary Clinton.

That respect and admiration between the two families extended to John F. Kennedy, Jr. His friends confirmed he had no interest in running for the U.S. Senate in New York to replace Daniel Patrick Moynihan if it meant running against Clinton. It would simply never happen, nor would he make any public statements to suggest he would ever oppose her. Joel Siegel of the *New York Daily News* interviewed some of Kennedy's friends the day after JFK, Jr.'s, plane went missing. They spoke anonymously to allow them to be quite candid about the issue of his potential entry into the Senate race. One friend put the timetable for his entry into politics "within five years," confirming the timetable mentioned above for a 2002 race for governor, and/or a 2004 run for the presidency. Another friend said he was considering the Senate run, "but the Hillary thing quickly ended it." Journalist Lawrence Leamer confirmed Kennedy's reluctance to go against Clinton in his book *Sons of Camelot*. He said that if Clinton wanted to run he would not fight her, and instead turn his political ambitions elsewhere. "He was too much of a gentleman," Leamer said.

There is one final point about why the Clintons would never want to assassinate JFK, Jr. Leamer points out that Kennedy's political magazine, *George,* never covered the Clinton sex scandal that plagued the second half of the Clinton presidency. Perhaps because of his father's similar behavior in this area, the younger Kennedy was willing to overlook this in President Clinton. Whatever the reason, the Clintons were thankful for the support that Kennedy demonstrated within the pages of *George*.

An anecdote during the Monica Lewinsky scandal best shows the support JFK, Jr., was giving to the Clintons, and closeness of the families. *People* reported this story on July 19, 2016.

"I was working in the White House when the Monica Lewinsky scandal was going on," Paul Begala, a one-time Clinton aide and current CNN political commentator, tells *People* in this week's issue. "I had a fax machine which very few people had the number to. It starts kicking in, and there's no cover sheet, just a page – it was John."

"It just said, 'Dear Mr. President, I sat under that desk – there's barely room for a 3-year-old, much less a 21-year-old intern. Cheers, J.K.' Typical John." Kennedy was, of course, referencing the famous image of him under the Oval Office desk taken while his father, John F. Kennedy was President. Clinton, who was being impeached on charges of perjury and obstruction of justice over his testimony about the Lewinsky affair during a sexual harassment lawsuit, laughed when he saw Kennedy's note.

"I showed the President and he laughed his butt off," says Begala. "It was so gutsy. And he was the perfect person to bring a little levity."

Therefore, it truly seems preposterous and counterintuitive to suspect that the Clintons could have conspired to kill this man given the mutual respect and admiration between these two families, as well as the fact that Kennedy posed no threat to Clinton, never having entered the Senate race, or having any intention to do so. In fact, the whole concept that the Clintons were behind Kennedy's assassination is more akin to misinformation, deliberately placed in the fringe media to distract attention from the real forces behind his assassination. It is reminiscent of theories for the JFK assassination that Fidel Castro, or the Russians, conspired to kill Kennedy, which have no real basis in fact. Removing the Clintons as possible conspirators is also enormously helpful to allow us to pin the blame on a much more likely force behind JFK, Jr.'s, assassination, namely the C.I.A.

# Chapter Two

# The C.I.A./Bush Motives

John F. Kennedy, Jr., posed a dual threat to the Bush family and the C.I.A. First, Kennedy was on the verge of exposing the role that the Bush family played in his father's assassination. As I will explore, the agency was more than willing to kill people to cover up this secret, as they had done in 1968 with the assassination of Robert Kennedy. Given this knowledge that George H. W. Bush played a role in the JFK assassination, JFK, Jr., had an intense interest in keeping another Bush out of the White House. A run for the presidency, or the vice presidency in 2000, or even 2004, would put him head to head against Texas Governor George W. Bush, who was beginning his campaign for the presidency in 1999. There would be no greater obstacle anywhere in the United States to four or eight years of a Bush presidency than John F. Kennedy, Jr. I will first establish the role the elder Bush played in the assassination of President Kennedy, and how he was in Dealey Plaza on the day of the shooting. Then I will demonstrate how JFK, Jr., became aware of this and was going to expose the truth just before his death in July 1999.

A third aspect to this case is the intergenerational hatred towards the Kennedys on the part of the C.I.A. that goes back to the botched Bay of Pigs in April 1961. We will explore how the timing of JFK, Jr.'s, assassination can be traced back to his father's administration's animosity towards the agency. Killing another Kennedy would be nothing new for this agency.

## A sudden interest in politics

Up until 1999, John F. Kennedy, Jr., had no interest in running for office, despite repeated speculation, and the knowledge that any such campaign would have been met with instant approval.

On July 19, 1988, at the age of 27, he gave a rousing speech to the Democratic National Convention, introducing his uncle, Senator Edward Kennedy. The speech was well received as he harkened back to his father's nomination in 1960. "Over a quarter of a century ago my father stood before you to accept the nomination for the presidency of the United States. So many of you came into public service because of him. In a very real sense because of you (meaning his uncle) he is with us still, and for that I am grateful," he said to a rapt audience in Atlanta. "I owe a special debt to the man his nephews and nieces call Teddy, not just because of what he means to me personally, but because of the causes he's carried on. He has shown that an unwavering commitment to the poor, to the elderly, to those without hope, regardless of faction or convention is the greatest reward of public service." It was a full two minutes before the assembled delegation would let his uncle give his speech, while many wiped tears from their eyes.

After this entry onto the public stage, many political observers felt the young Kennedy heir to the throne would plan a run for a Congressional seat. The age to run for Congress is 25 years-old according to the Constitution, and the next chance to run for Congress would be in 1990 when he would be 29 years-old. This would follow the path set by his father, who won a Massachusetts Congressional seat in 1946 at age 29. It was not to be. Kennedy spent the next 11 years denying any interest in running for office. Even later that year when he was named *People Magazine's* Sexiest Man Alive, he deflected these rumors, as did members of his family. Senator Kennedy said he believed that his nephew would one day be involved in public affairs. "Not necessarily running for office, but trying to make some sort of contribution." Cousin Robert Kennedy, Jr., said, "He has a tremendous sense of duty and responsibility. Whenever any of the cousins need help on one of their [charity] projects, John always participates."

This attitude had not changed five years later in 1993. In an interview with *Vogue Magazine*, Kennedy indicated that he was still no closer to being a politician. He admitted that he had thought about running for office 'a lot,'" but added that he was not ready. "Once you run for office, you're in it," he said. "Sort of like going into the military you'd better be damn sure that it is what you want to do and that the rest of your life is set up to accommodate that. It takes a certain toll on your personality and on your family life."

Three years later, Kennedy was still deflecting and turning down presidential chatter, this time in the presence of real estate developer Donald Trump. Michael Berman, a Kennedy partner at *George* magazine, was with JFK, Jr., at Trump's Mar a Lago estate in Florida along with a group of advertisers when the talk turned to politics. Kennedy joked that the Trump estate was far more glamorous than the Kennedy family's compound in Hyannisport, Massachusetts, where JFK, Jr., was headed to on the night of his fated flight.

"I think you should be asking those questions of Donald," he said, according to Berman. "He'd clearly have the most extravagant winter White House," Kennedy said, who at that time was 35 years-old, the first year of eligibility to run for the White House.

Then these denials of any interest in running for office came to an abrupt end in 1999. Why would this man who consistently wished to stay out of politics, despite repeated chances to enter the fray, suddenly change his mind in 1999? Up until then he was satisfied with life as an editor. Can we be certain that 1999, and not any earlier was when he finally decided to enter politics? One key sign that he was ready to enter politics that is often overlooked is that he was selling his magazine. His business partner and friend Gary Ginsberg confirmed this. "That last night he was very focused on two things: finding a buyer for *George*, and his political future," he said.

As will be explored below, by this point in his life, JFK, Jr., had concluded that George Herbert Walker Bush had played some role in his father's assassination, and helped cover up the truth while C.I.A. director in the 1970s. Kennedy was exploring his options about what to do with this information. His initial attempt to tell the world about this, was the name of his magazine. He also was planning to run an expose in his magazine about Bush's role in the assassination. The power of the presidency could also help reopen an investigation into his father's assassination, as well as his uncle's. John F. Kennedy, Jr., would therefore probably not have reacted well to the news on March 2, 1999, that Texas Governor George W. Bush was forming an exploratory committee to run for president. Bush made it official when he announced his candidacy on June 14, 1999, one month before Kennedy's plane crash. The very idea of another Bush presidency must have been anathema to Kennedy. He must have felt compelled to try to stop this, either by making plans to run for president, and/or to expose the truth behind the JFK assassination. Trying to block four to eight years in the White House for the son of his father's killer must have been a deciding factor that brought Kennedy into the world of politics, and out of the world of publishing.

Therefore, I need to examine what evidence there is that George Herbert Walker Bush played some role in the assassination of John F. Kennedy. Having established that, I will have to show that John F. Kennedy, Jr., was aware of this information in 1999, and ready to go public with it, just like his uncle Robert Kennedy had conducted his own investigation, and had concluded that the C.I.A. had murdered JFK. It is no coincidence they met with the same fate.

## George

Was George H. W. Bush working for the C.I.A. in 1963? Journalist and historian Joseph McBride has done some essential work linking Bush to the C.I.A and the Kennedy assassination. He started as a volunteer for JFK's Wisconsin primary campaign, where Kennedy scored a decisive early victory over Hubert Humphry with 53% of the vote, on April 5, 1960. McBride began researching the assassination in 1963 and eventually authored a book, released in 2013, titled, *Into the Nightmare: My Search for the Killers of President John F. Kennedy and Officer J. D. Tippit.* Through the Freedom of Information Act, McBride, who is now a professor at San Francisco State University, uncovered an F.B.I. document in 1988 that confirms the fact that George Bush was a C.I.A. agent in 1963. The memo, dated Nov. 29, 1963, was written by J. Edgar Hoover, the director of the F.B.I., and sent to the director of the Bureau of Intelligence and Research at the Department of State. According to their website, the "INR's primary mission is to harness intelligence to serve U.S. diplomacy. Secretary of State George Marshall established INR in 1947. INR is a direct descendant of the Office of Strategic Services Research Department and the oldest civilian intelligence element in the U.S. Government." The Office of Strategic Services of course was the forerunner to the C.I.A., where most of its recruits came from. As a key member of the intelligence community, on regular basis, the INR shares information with the National Security Council, the C.I.A., and the F.B.I. In 1963, the director of the INR was Roger Hilsman, whose name Hoover oddly leaves off the document. This might have been a sly insult to Hilsman, a friend and confidant to the dead president. JFK relied on Hilsman to give him unfiltered advice. He also was not afraid to take on the military, and helped craft JFK's withdrawal policy from Vietnam that was supposed to return all troops home by 1965.

"So it was a hopeless situation and Kennedy came to this conclusion and, you know, as I said, and his decision was to get the American advisers out, there were only sixteen thousand five hundred there and he removed the first one thousand and had an approved plan for removing the rest within a matter of two or three months. It was hopeless," Hilsman said. Author

David Halberstam, who discussed the Vietnam War in his book, *The Best and the Brightest*, said about Hilsman, "He had probably made more enemies than anyone else in the upper levels of government, partly because of the viewpoints he represented, partly because of the brashness with which he presented them."

Hoover's motives remain unclear for why he left Hilsman's name off this document. The substance of the memo is to reassure Hilsman that Cubans in Miami would not be using the assassination as an excuse invade Cuba, "believing that the assassination of President Kennedy might herald a change in U.S. policy, which is not true." There was "stunned disbelief" among the Cuban population, and Hoover was confident to report that there would be no sanctioned, nor unsanctioned invasion of Cuba by the C.I.A. Hoover finished the memo by saying where this information came from. "The substance of the forgoing information was orally furnished by Mr. George Bush of the Central Intelligence Agency and Captain William Edwards of the Defense Intelligence Agency on November 23, 1963, by Mr. V. T. Forsyth of this Bureau." Interestingly, the part where it mentions Bush is very hard to read on the document. An intimate knowledge of C.I.A. plans (or lack of plans) to invade Cuba, suggests at least some level of security clearance to be able to confidently report this to the F.B.I. director, one day after the assassination. So, this document not only proves that Bush was in the C.I.A., but evidently, he had been in the agency for quite some time. *The New York Times* on July 11, 1988, leaked a story about this memo under the headline "63 F.B.I. Memo Ties Bush to Intelligence Agency." Bush and his surrogates absurdly claimed that this was a different George Bush, a certain George William Bush, who also worked for the C.I.A. This is not true. George William Bush explained in an affidavit on September 21, 1988, that he could not have been the same George Bush mentioned in this memo from Hoover. This *New York Times* story was less than two months before George Herbert Walker Bush was elected president. It is telling that Bush would be so insistent on lying about his membership in the agency, even after it became clear that he must have been the George Bush mentioned in the F.B.I. memo. Why the need to make sure his name was not connected to the Kennedy assassination, even after it was clear he could not blame this on George William Bush due to the following affidavit reproduced below?

I, George William Bush, a resident of Alexandria, Virginia, do hereby state under oath as follows:

My name is George William Bush. I reside in Alexandria, Virginia.

From September 1963 to February 1964 I worked at the Central Intelligence Agency headquarters.

My job responsibility was as a junior watch officer.

As a junior watch officer I was part of a team of three or four persons on watch on any particular shift.

I was the junior person on duty at the time of the John F. Kennedy assassination.

I have carefully reviewed the F.B.I. memorandum to the Director, Bureau of Intelligence and Research, Department of State, dated November 29, 1963, which mentions a Mr. George Bush of the Central Intelligence Agency (attached hereto as exhibit 1).

I do not recognize the contents of the memorandum as information furnished to me orally or otherwise during the time I was at the C.I.A. In fact, during my time at the C.I.A. I did not receive any oral communications from any government agency of any nature whatsoever. I did not receive any information relating to the Kennedy assassination during my time at the C.I.A. from the F.B.I.

Based on the above, it is my conclusion, that I am not the Mr. George Bush of the Central Intelligence Agency referred to in the memorandum.

A second F.B.I memo from the day of the assassination is equally fascinating because it allows us to follow Bush's movements on the day of the assassination, and place him in Dallas by his own admission. Here is the memo.

TO: SAC, HOUSTON DATE: 11-22-63
FROM: SA GRAHAM W. KITCHEL
SUBJECT: UNKNOWN SUBJECT; ASSASSINATION OF PRESIDENT JOHN F. KENNEDY
At 1:45 p.m. Mr. GEORGE H. W. BUSH, President of the Zapata Off-Shore Drilling Company, Houston, Texas, residence 5525 Briar, Houston, telephonically furnished the following information to writer by long distance telephone call from Tyler, Texas.
BUSH stated that he wanted to be kept confidential but wanted to furnish hearsay that he recalled hearing in recent weeks, the day and source unknown. He stated that one JAMES PARROTT has been talking of killing the President when he comes to Houston. BUSH stated that PARROTT is possibly a student at the University of Houston and is active in political matters in this area. He stated that he felt Mrs. FAWLEY, telephone number SU 2-5239, or ARLINE SMITH, telephone number JA 9-9194 of the Harris County Republican Party Headquarters would be able to furnish additional information regarding the identity of PARROTT.
BUSH stated that he was proceeding to Dallas, Texas, would remain in the Sheraton-Dallas Hotel and return to his residence on 11-23-63. His office telephone number is CA 2-0395.

Special Agent Kitchel reported this to the Strategic Air Command (SAC) in Houston, part of the president's military protection for his Texas visit. Bush seeks to provide himself with an alibi by saying he was in Tyler, Texas, during the time of the assassination. He also pathetically tries laying the blame for the assassination on a sign painter who was no more than an ardent GOP supporter, and had a strong alibi of being at home with his family during the assassination. As we will establish later, photographic evidence proves that Bush was in Dealey Plaza during the time of the assassination. He could easily have made the short flight from Dallas to Tyler, Texas, to make a phone call around 1:45 p.m. He also could have just routed the call through another location, or pretended to call from there. He also admits he is going back to the Sheraton Dallas Hotel and remain there overnight. He obviously had been to this hotel earlier in the day, or the previous day, otherwise he wouldn't have had such confidence in securing a room at that specific hotel unless he had already been checked in. Telling the F.B.I. that he was in Tyler, Texas, at 1:45 p.m. and blaming the assassination on an obviously innocent man just makes him look guiltier. Author and historian Russ Baker has done the definitive work establishing Bush's timeline of events from November 21, 1963, to November 22, 1963, none of which Bush claimed he could remember happening. Baker writes in his book *Family of Secrets: The Bush Dynasty, America's Invisible Government and the Hidden History of the Last Fifty Years*:

> On the evening of November 21, 1963, Poppy Bush spoke to a gathering of the American Association of Oil Drilling Contractors (AAODC) at the Sheraton Hotel in Dallas. Since Joe Zeppa himself was a former president of AAODC, it is likely that he attended that gathering. It is also likely that both Zeppa and the Bushes spent the night in Dallas – and that they were in Dallas the next morning: the day that Kennedy was assassinated.

This brings us to the vexing question of Poppy's motive in calling the F.B.I. at 1.45 p.m. on November 22, to identify James Parrott as a possible suspect in the president's murder, and to mention that he, George H. W. Bush, happened to be in Tyler, Texas. He told the F.B.I. that he expected to spend the night of November 22 at the Sheraton Hotel in Dallas – but instead, after flying to Dallas on Zeppa's plane, he left again almost immediately on a commercial flight to Houston. Why state that he expected to spend the night at the Dallas Sheraton if he was not planning to stay? Perhaps this was to create a little confusion, to blur the fact that he had *already* stayed at the hotel – the night before. Anyone inquiring would learn that Bush was in Tyler at the time of the assassination and *planned* to stay in Dallas afterward, but canceled his plan following JFK's death.

Blaming James Parrott for the assassination played a key role in Bush's plans on the day of the assassination, as Baker further explains in his book. Bush knew Parrott personally, as Brown explains, so Bush would have known he posed no threat to the president. Parrott's mother also provided her son with a strong alibi. "She advised [James Parrott] had been home all day helping her care for her son Gary Wayne Parrott whom they brought home from the hospital yesterday. Mrs. Parrott's other son could not help, because he was in jail. She also mentioned another person who could provide an alibi, according to Baker. Mrs. Parrott advised that shortly after 1:00 p.m. a Mr. Reynolds came by their home to advise them of the death of President Kennedy, and talked to her son James Parrott about painting some signs at Republican Headquarters on Waugh Drive." Brown also revealed that F.B.I. agent Graham Kitchel was a close friend of the Bush family. They met through Kitchel's brother, George, who was also in the Texas oil business like George Bush. "In summary, then, Bush called in a pointless tip about an innocent fellow to an F.B.I. agent whom he knew, and whom he knew could be counted on to file a report on this tip – out of what may have been hundreds of calls, some of them not even worthy of documenting. And, after a cursory investigation, the tip was confirmed as useless. But the call itself was hardly without value. It established for the record, if anyone asked, that Poppy Bush was not in Dallas when Kennedy was shot. By pointing to a seemingly harmless man who lived with his mother, Bush appeared to establish his own Pollyannaish ignorance of the larger plot."

The night before the assassination, Bush was likely in attendance at a gathering at the Dallas mansion of Clint Murchison, Sr. People in attendance included Lyndon Johnson, J. Edgar Hoover, Richard Nixon, and many fellow Texas oil magnates who were friends of the host. Murchison, like Bush, was part of the small but wealthy group of oil men in Texas who hated President Kennedy's policy toward something called the Oil Depletion Allowance. As a U.S. Senator from Texas, Johnson was a major supporter of the Oil Depletion Allowance which allowed oil companies to avoid taxes on the wealth they and their families obtained from oil. Robert Bryce explained in his book, *Cronies: Oil, the Bushes, and the Rise of Texas, America's Superstate*, "Numerous studies showed that the oilmen were getting a tax break that was unprecedented in American business. While other businessmen had to pay taxes on their income regardless of what they sold, the oilmen got special treatment." Bryce gave an example of how the oil depreciation allowance works. "An oilman drills a well that costs $100,000. He finds a reservoir containing $10,000,000 worth of oil. The well produces $1 million worth of oil per year for ten years. In the very first year, thanks to the depletion allowance, the oilman could deduct 27.5 per cent, or $275,000, of that $1 million in income from his taxable income. Thus, in just one year, he's deducted nearly three times his initial investment. But the depletion allowance continues to pay off. For each of the next nine years, he gets to continue taking the

$275,000 depletion deduction. By the end of the tenth year, the oilman has deducted $2.75 million from his taxable income, even though his initial investment was only $100,000." This benefited all the oilmen in Texas, including Murchison and Bush.

President Kennedy had other ideas about the Oil Depletion Allowance. According to JFK assassination researcher, John Simkin, "On 16th October, 1962, Kennedy was able to persuade Congress to pass an act that removed the distinction between repatriated profits and profits reinvested abroad. While this law applied to the industry as a whole, it especially affected the oil companies. It was estimated that as a result of this legislation, wealthy oilmen saw a fall in their earnings on foreign investment from 30 per cent to 15 per cent." Kennedy then went further during his State of the Union Address, on January 17, 1963, to wage a full attack on the ODA. "President Kennedy presented his proposals for tax reform. This included relieving the tax burdens of low-income and elderly citizens. Kennedy also claimed he wanted to remove special privileges and loopholes. He even said he wanted to do away with the oil depletion allowance. It is estimated that the proposed removal of the oil depletion allowance would result in a loss of around $300 million a year to Texas oilmen." In presenting the tax reform proposal, Kennedy said that "no one industry should be permitted to obtain an undue advantage over all others."

This meeting at the Murchison mansion in north Dallas lasted late into the evening of November 21, 1963, so there is no question Bush could have paid a visit there after giving his speech at the Sheraton. On Wednesday, November 20, 1963, an advertisement under "Club Activities" was published in the *Dallas Morning News* stating that George Bush, president, Zapata Off-Shore Co., would be speaking for the American Association of Oilwell Drilling contractors at 6:30 p.m., the next day at the Sheraton-Dallas Hotel. The 6:30 p.m. start time would have given him plenty of time to reach north Dallas for this meeting that has become known as a type of "ratification meeting," where final instructions on the plan to assassinate the president, and stage the cover up, were fashioned out. As Lyndon Johnson was leaving the mansion late that night, he was confident enough to tell his mistress, Madeline Duncan Brown, who was also there, that "those god damn Kennedys will never embarrass me again. That is no threat. That is a promise." He repeated the threat in a phone call to her the following morning, just hours before the assassination. She wrote about this in her 1997 book, *Texas in the Morning*. JFK assassination filmmaker Nigel Turner extensively covers the existence of this meeting, and the proof for it in part nine of "The Men Who Killed Kennedy." He interviews Brown, as well as May Newman, a seamstress for Clint's wife, Virginia. Newman confirmed that the Murchison chauffeur drove Hoover back and forth from the airport, and that the stingy F.B.I. director stiffed him on the tip for both times.

There is plenty of photographic evidence pinning Bush inside Dealey Plaza. YouTuber and JFK assassination expert researcher Saintly Oswald suggests that Bush may have been next to Murchison on the north side of Houston Street, with Bush apparently holding a camera in his hands, or perhaps a signaling device, just as the presidential motorcade was passing by. This is just a few steps from the entry to the Dal-Tex Building. The Murchison – Bush photo is just one of many images that show Bush in Dealey Plaza that afternoon. A second photo was taken after the assassination when Dallas Police officers began to gather in front of the Texas School Book Depository. Bush is shown furtively looking away from the camera with his hands in his pockets, his receding hairline clearly visible. A third photo shows him leaving Dealey Plaza with C.I.A. agent Edward Landsdale, who was also seen escorting the infamous "three tramps" out of the plaza, one of whom allegedly was C.I.A. agent E. Howard Hunt. Bush being with Landsdale further confirms his connection to the C.I.A. Landsdale's role in the agency was often to function in a support capacity, to take care of the aftermath of an assassination. In this case, he saw to it that his agents safely left the plaza after the mission was completed, in this case Bush, Hunt, and the other two "tramps." He also performed a similar role in the aftermath of the execution of Mary Pinchot Meyer, the ex-wife of C.I.A. agent Cord Meyer, disposing of her journal after her suspicious death as we will discuss later in part one.

New Orleans District Attorney Jim Garrison also turned up evidence of the presence of George H. W. Bush in Dealey Plaza during Garrison's C.I.A.-focused investigation as well. Deputy Sheriff Roger Craig told Garrison twelve arrests were made in Dealey Plaza after the assassination. One arrest was made by R. E. Vaughn of the Dallas Police Department. He took into custody a man running out of the Dal-Tex Building, who said he was "an independent oil operator from Houston, Texas." The prisoner was taken by Vaughn to the Dallas Police Department, and that was the last he saw of him. Craig told Garrison that no mug shot, interview, fingerprints, or name was in existence of this mystery oil man. "Independent oil operator from Houston" was always George H. W. Bush's C.I.A cover. Afterward, Craig said that two police officers escorted him out of the police department to the jeers of the waiting crowd. Bush was put in a police car and he was driven away, right back to Dealey Plaza, where he was photographed with Edward Lansdale. It is possible that Bush used his one phone call to the F.B.I. at 1:45 p.m. from inside Dallas Police Headquarters, pretending he was calling from Tyler. It is possible that the call to his F.B.I. friend Kitchel was what got him released so quickly as well. Kitchel probably vouched for him, that Bush was on assignment, accounting for the lack of a mug shot, fingerprints, or interview notes. The call may not have even happened at 1:45 p.m. Kitchel, as we established was a Bush confidant and likely would have been willing to put down that the call took place at 1:45 p.m., long after the assassination, if that is what Bush wanted him to do. It is also equally likely that any record of a call from Bush to Kitchel would have been purged from any records of phone calls coming in and out of Dallas Police Headquarters that day.

What was Bush doing in Dealey Plaza, now that we have established that he was there? Keep in mind if he was doing nothing sinister there would be no need to lie about his presence, invent a fake alibi, or blame the assassination on someone else. He could easily have said, like many other Texans, that he simply came to see the president, or fellow Republican John Connally, and no one would have questioned this. This indicates therefore that he must have been there to perform some function. JFK assassination historians Jim Fetzer, and Richard Hooke, have done extensive research on the Bush connection to the JFK assassination. Their collective conclusion after years of investigation is that Bush was in Dallas to coordinate the C.I.A. hit team, and make sure the shooters got in position. Bush was placed with one of the teams in and around the Dal-Tex Building behind the motorcade, where Kennedy's back wound originated from. This accounts for Bush leaving the Dal-Tex Building, and subsequently being arrested leaving its premises. "Extensive, meticulous and detailed examination of the medical, ballistic and eyewitness testimony supports the conclusion that JFK was hit four times – once in the back (from behind); once in the throat (from in front); and twice in the head (once in the back of the head from behind and once in the right temple from the right/front)," said Fetzer. "None of those shots appear to have been fired from the 6th floor "assassin's lair" but three from the Dal-Tex, where the acoustics were such that they sounded as though they could have been fired from the Texas School Book Depository. Richard's study suggests that GHWB was at that window of the Dal-Tex."

Obviously, such an important assignment would not have been given to someone new in the agency. Bush was 39 years-old in 1963, not exactly fresh out of college. Hooke also did extensive research proving that Bush had worked for the C.I.A. for many years, culled from the ranks of the Skull and Bones Society which he had joined while attending Yale University. Bush graduated in 1948, just months after the C.I.A. was formed in September 1947. The agency liked to recruit members from secret societies like the Skull and Bones in its early days because these men knew how to keep a secret and remain loyal to a group. Russ Baker recounted this in his book, *Family of Secrets*.

"Yale has always been the agency's biggest feeder," recalled C.I.A. officer Osborne Day (class of '43), "In my Yale class alone there were thirty-five guys in the agency." Bush's father, Prescott, was on the university's board, and the school was crawling with faculty serving as recruiters for the intelligence services . . . Yale's society's boys were the cream of the crop, and could keep secrets to boot. And no secret society was more suited to the spy establishment than Skull and Bones, for which Poppy Bush, like his father, was tapped in his junior year. Established in 1832, Skull and Bones is the oldest secret society at Yale, and thus at least theoretically entrusted its membership with a more comprehensive body of secrets than any other campus group. When Bush entered Yale, the university was welcoming back countless veterans of the OSS to its faculty. Bush, with naval intelligence work already under his belt by the time he arrived at Yale, would have been a particularly prime candidate for recruitment.

Journalist Kris Millegan has done research on the Skull and Bones Society and its connections to the intelligence community. Millegan interviewed Gaddis Smith, a history professor at Yale, who said, "Yale has influenced the Central Intelligence Agency more than any other university, giving the C.I.A. the atmosphere of a class reunion." It wasn't long before Bush was recruiting fellow Skull members into the agency, such as Sloan Coffin,

Jr., according to Millegan. JFK assassination researcher, Hooke discovered that Bush went on to have a key role in many C.I.A. operations in the ensuing years between his recruitment and the J.F.K assassination. "He and his wife Barbara moved to Houston where he ran an offshore oil drilling business, Zapata Offshore Co., which was a C.I.A. front company with rigs located all over the world, making it very convenient for him to vanish for weeks at a time on C.I.A. business where no one would suspect what he was doing," Hooke said. "Bush was a major organizer and recruiter for the Bay of Pigs invasion, which was codenamed Operation ZAPATA. Col. Fletcher Prouty, former Pentagon high ranking official, who was the basis for the 'Col. X' character in Oliver Stone's 'JFK,' obtained two Navy ships for the operation that were repainted to non-Navy colors and then renamed HOUSTON and BARBARA."

Millegan, the Skulls and Bones expert, also pointed out that many of Bush's recruits for the Cuban invasion came from Miami, from disaffected Cubans. When Kennedy refused to invade Cuba, or provide additional air support during the Bay of Pigs Invasion, they felt betrayed. Bush's involvement in Miami recruitment for the Cuban attack further confirms he was the Bush named in the F.B.I. document that discussed Cuban reaction in Miami to the assassination because he knew the area quite well.

If Bush was coordinating an assassination hit team, it is possible he made sure to take with him to Dallas at least one of his disaffected Cubans who took part in the Bay of Pigs Invasion to witness the assassination. This brings us to the story of the so-called "dark complected man." Orlando Bosch was a Cuban exile, and a contract killer for the C.I.A. He has long been suspected by many assassination researchers of being the "dark complected man." This person acted bizarrely just as the fatal shots were delivered to the president. He died in Miami on April 27, 2011, at age 85. DCM was standing next to the "Umbrella

Man" on the curb right next to Kennedy's limousine. These two would likely have been the last people the president saw in his life. Perhaps that was the gruesome intent from the plotters. As the motorcade carrying JFK approached these two, the umbrella man raised his black umbrella, pumped it, and twirled it several times. Simultaneously, the DCM raised his arm in an apparent signal, as the president reacted to being shot in the throat. One theory put forward by many assassination researchers is that these series of motions were meant to show JFK why he was being killed. The umbrella was a symbol the president's controversial decision to not provide an "umbrella" of air support during the failed Bay of Pigs Invasion.

As the car drove away, and Dealey Plaza descended into chaos, the pair calmly sat down next to each other. DCM then got up and appeared to talk into a walkie talkie that had been tucked into his back pocket.

There is further evidence that Bush hand-picked this man to be part of the assassination team, and it comes from events later in his life when Bush seemed obsessed with keeping Bosch out of jail, probably in return for keeping his mouth shut about what he knew about the assassination, and Bush's connection to it. Many key people involved with the assassination rarely lived into their 80s, like Bosch did. Orlando Bosch was the head of the Coordination of United Revolutionary Organizations, which the F.B.I. under Hoover described as "an anti-Castro terrorist umbrella organization." Former U.S. Attorney General Dick Thornburgh said Bosch was an "unrepentant terrorist," who likely took part in the bombing of a Cuban civilian airliner on October 6, 1976, in which all 73 people on the plane were killed. On board were members of a Cuban fencing team, and five North Koreans. The plan for the bombing was hatched at a 1976 meeting in Washington, during which time Bush was C.I.A director. In attendance were Bosch, Luis Posada Carriles, and DINA agent Michael Townley. The C.I.A. plan to assassinate

Chilean prime minister Orlando Letelier was likely formulated here as well. Letelier died in a car bombing on September 21, 1976, in Washington, D.C. Letelier was a vocal opponent of Chilean dictator Gen. Augusto Pinochet, a C.I.A. puppet ruler. Later that year, Costa Rica tried to extradite Bosch to put him on trial, but this effort was blocked by C.I.A. Director George H. W. Bush. Later when he became president, Bush granted Bosch safe haven status within the United States, to shield him from any prosecution.

Robert J. Groden in his book *The Killing of a President*, also reported when Bush left the presidency in 1993 he took with him documents related to the Kennedy assassination that stayed "in his possession," countermanding an order from the 1992 John F. Kennedy Assassination Records Review Act that demands the release of such documents. He likely obtained them at some point during his time as director of the C.I.A. from 1976 until President Jimmy Carter took office in 1977. Bush was appointed director by Warren Commission member, Gerald Ford. Groden also reported that Bush used his time as director to make sure the official media stayed away from inquiring into the assassination. "In February 1976, prior to the formation of the House Assassinations Committee later that year, C.I.A. Director George Bush called for a meeting with (CBS Chairman William) Paley, and (the president of CBS News Richard) Salant to gain support for the C.I.A.'s policy of 'burying the past,'" said Groden. "One of the CBS executives told Bush, 'we protect ours, you protect yours,' when dealing with C.I.A. contacts within the CBS news organization, as well as with those stringers working for other national publications."

Bush also made sure that the C.I.A. did little to help the House Select Committee on Assassinations that was formed in September 1976 to investigate the assassinations of JFK, and Martin Luther King, Jr. By then, Bush had been director for nine months. Bush made it the policy of the agency that they would only share documents with the Congress unless they specifically asked for them. This then gave the agency time to redact anything they wanted from these documents, or just outright refuse to release large sections of documents. It was not until May 2013 under President Obama that 175 batches of documents that the C.I.A. withheld since 1976 finally were released. However, 1,100 documents remained classified that relate to a host of names attached to the JFK assassination conspiracy. Here is a summary of the relevant files from jfkfacts.org:

E. Howard Hunt, former Watergate burglar, who made a video for his son late in life in which he insinuated that C.I.A. officers had plotted against JFK's life. The C.I.A. retains six files on Hunt's operations containing 332 pages of material.

David Phillips, the chief of anti-Castro operations in 1963, who oversaw the surveillance of Lee Harvey Oswald in Mexico City six weeks before JFK's assassination and who gave contradictory and evasive testimony to investigators. Phillips also organized a C.I.A.-sponsored assassination conspiracy to kill a top general in Chile in 1970, according to the non-profit National Security Archive at George Washington University. The C.I.A. retains four files containing 606 pages of material on Phillips.

William K. Harvey, the one-time chief of the C.I.A.'s assassination program who was known for his hatred of the Kennedys. Harvey's biographer, a former C.I.A. officer turned *Newsweek* correspondent, devoted a whole chapter of his book to examining allegations that Harvey was involved in JFK's murder. The C.I.A. retains one file on Harvey containing 123 pages of material.

David Sanchez Morales, deputy chief of the C.I.A.'s Miami station in 1963, who later boasted of being involved in JFK's death, according to a friend. "We took care of that SOB," he reportedly said. The C.I.A. is keeping secret a 61-page administrative file on Morales.

George Joannides, chief of psychological warfare operations in Miami in 1963, whose agents in the Cuban exile community took the lead in publicizing Lee Harvey Oswald's pro-Castro activities before and after JFK was killed. In 1978, Joannides misled congressional investigators about his role in the events of 1963. In 1981, he received a C.I.A. medal for his actions. The C.I.A. is keeping 295 documents about Joannides secret in their entirety.

These files could have been shared to the House Select Committee on Assassinations, but Director George H. W. Bush chose secrecy instead. Further complicity of Bush's actions in the C.I.A. and his complicity in planning the assassination comes from evidence uncovered by historian, and assassination researcher Rodney Stich. In his book *Defrauding America,* he writes about a "deep-cover C.I.A. officer" assigned to a counter-intelligence unit, code-named Pegasus. This unit "had tape-recordings of plans to assassinate Kennedy" from a tap on the phone of J. Edgar Hoover. The people on the tapes were "[Nelson] Rockefeller, Allen Dulles, [Lyndon] Johnson of Texas, George Bush, and J. Edgar Hoover." Notice that these were many of the same people at the Murchinson "ratification meeting," mentioned above.

Having established that George Herbert Walker Bush played at least some role in the assassination of John F. Kennedy, and that he certainly took part in the cover up, it is necessary to prove that John F. Kennedy, Jr., knew about these facts, and was going to expose the truth behind the assassination. Even if it was not true that Bush played a key role in the killing of his father, if

JFK, Jr. believed that is was true that would be all that would be needed to seek justice, and prevent another Bush from becoming president. An exploration of the evidence begins with the name of his magazine, *George*.

## The Burden of Knowledge

John F. Kennedy, Jr., told everyone who he thought killed his father, by hiding the answer in plain sight. The name of his magazine, *George*, told the world who was behind the assassination of John F. Kennedy. The timing for the sudden interest in becoming a publisher is key to this whole tragic story. Kennedy was planning on using the magazine as a platform to expose the truth of his father's slaying. However, he had to wait for concrete proof that could lead to an indictment. In September 1995, when the magazine debuted, Bush would have been nearing the end of his second term had he won reelection, so he was still very much alive and well. What also may have lit a fire under John F. Kennedy, Jr., was making sure that another Bush did not enter the White House. We noted above that when Governor George W. Bush announced his intention to run for the presidency, in March 1999, Kennedy quickly began exploring his own options for running for public office. We can trace this concern about the younger Bush back to 1995 as well. On January 17, 1995, George W. Bush became the 46th governor of Texas. 10 months later, *George* magazine was hitting the newsstands everywhere.

On the day of JFK, Jr.'s, plane crash, the Bush campaign for president made a stunning announcement that showed how confident Bush was in winning the nomination and the presidency, even at that early stage of the campaign. *The New York Times* reported on July 16, 1999:

Gov. George W. Bush declared today that he would not accept Federal matching funds because of his enormous

$37 million campaign war chest, giving him the capacity to far outspend his Republican Presidential rivals in the 2000 election, especially in early and pivotal primaries and caucuses... By refusing to accept $16.5 million in matching funds from taxpayers, Mr. Bush, with more than $30 million in cash reserves, will not be restricted by a spending limit of nearly $40 million that applies to candidates who accept matching funds in the primaries. More important, both of Mr. Bush's chief Democratic rivals, Vice President Al Gore and former Senator Bill Bradley of New Jersey, who are accepting matching funds, will probably reach the spending limit by the spring of 2000. But Mr. Bush would still have ample amounts of money left to spend through the summer conventions.

According to JFK assassination expert John Hankey, George W. Bush was nowhere to be found on the day of Kennedy's plane crash, as well as for the next three days, even though his campaign for president was in full swing since June 14. "Karen Hughes, the head of the Bush campaign, was unable to tell reporters where Bush was, what he was doing, or when he would be back to respond to their questions about the death of JFK, Jr. – this at the height of the 2000 campaign. And Bush stayed missing for 3 days," said Hankey. "It turns out he was spotted at the Bohemian Grove celebrating JFK, Jr.'s death. Additional screwiness: the year before and the year following JFK, Jr.'s, death, the Bushes were open and casual about their participation at the Bohemian Grove, and their presence was treated openly and casually in the press. In fact, (Richard) Cheney announced that he was going to be the vice-presidential candidate from the Bohemian Grove in 2000."

The Bohemian Grove has long been speculated as a place where conspiracies are hatched and the Illuminati meet every year to control the world order. Bohemian Grove covers 2,700-acres over a wide campground in Monte Rio, California.

Every year in the middle of July the Bohemian Grove hosts a two-week encampment of some of the most prominent people in the world. The activities, hierarchy of leadership, and closed meetings have all the trappings of a cult, or secret society. Was the assassination of John F. Kennedy, Jr., planned for the middle of July so that the Bush family and other conspirators could privately celebrate the success of the plot? That seems to be what Hankey has concluded. According to the UK *Guardian*, and author G. William Domhoff in his book, The *Bohemian Grove and Other Retreats*, the Bush family are frequent guests at the Grove.

By the spring of 1999, Kennedy was positioning himself for some momentous life changes. First, he would run for office, likely for New York State governor, or vice president. Second, he would find and expose the truth behind his father's death. Third, he would do what he could to keep another Bush out of the White House. Surely, the truth that the senior Bush was behind the JFK assassination would destroy any hope for the younger Bush to even sniff the White House. There is also some evidence that George W. Bush accompanied his father to Dallas, or was flown there, to witness the assassination. JFK assassination researcher Richard M. Hooke is convinced that GWB was indeed there. A picture taken at around 12:35 p.m. shows a confused looking young man wandering near one of the police motorcycles. Hooke says it matches the description of the younger Bush in every way. The young man may have been wondering where his father was, given the fact that the older Bush had just been taken into police custody. At the time, George W. Bush was attending the prestigious Phillips Academy in Andover, Massachusetts. There would be virtually no obstacles to getting his son to Dealey Plaza to join him to witness the assassination if the elder Bush wanted to. The family certainly could afford to dispatch a private charter plane to bring young George to Dallas, or even use Joe Zeppa's private craft that was used to allegedly take Bush to Tyler, Texas, after the assassination to establish his alibi. There were certainly no financial obstacles for this wealthy oil family, or logistical ones given their access to private transportation. The school would have no objection either to Bush taking his son for the weekend to miss a day or two of classes, given the fact that he was a financial contributor to the school, and an alumnus, having graduated president of his class in 1942. The elder Bush could have even said he wanted to keep his son through the upcoming Thanksgiving break for family reasons and the administration would probably have raised no objections.

However, we can fashion two key points from his potential presence, if in fact George W. Bush was in Dallas that day. First, he knew his father was part of the conspiracy. He would have either overtly or directly concluded this by witnessing the assassination, either because his father told him, or he concluded that being pulled out of school and flown to Dallas to witness the assassination. This would have been just too much of a coincidence. Secondly, if he deliberately chose to have his teenage son witness the president get his head blown off, it speaks to the level of hatred that Bush must have felt towards the Kennedys, and a certain amount of sadism that he was giving into here. If George W. Bush was there, it seems likely he knew exactly the role his father was playing in this. He likely would have rarely left his side, and may have even met the assassins if Bush was coordinating the hit team. In the chaos following the shooting it does seem possible that he could have gotten separated from his father. It is worth noting that if George W. Bush was in fact in Dallas that day, he appears to be the only child that the elder Bush chose to bring to the assassination, grooming this future president even at this young age, in his own image. In the final analysis though, placing George W. Bush in Dealey Plaza amounts to little in the whole scheme of things. Whether he was there or not does nothing to add or detract from the older Bush's role in the assassination, or JFK, Jr.'s, desire to expose the truth.

Therefore, let us try to establish that JFK, Jr., was in fact researching his father's death. The most credible source and most interesting lead was brought up by Don Jeffries, the author of *Hidden History: An Expose of Modern Crimes, Conspiracies, and Cover-Ups in American Politics.* He pointed out that Kennedy's high school girlfriend, Meg Azzoni, had a lot to reveal about JFK, Jr.'s, mindset when he interviewed her. Kennedy and Azzoni dated when they attended Phillips Academy in the late 1970s, ironically the same school that the Bush family sent their children to. It was here that the young Kennedy began to show an interest in finding out the truth behind the assassination. Was Kennedy able to obtain the attendance records of young George W. Bush for November 1963? Even later in his life, as an alumnus he probably had enough connections at the school to find out if George W. Bush was at Phillips Academy on November 22, 1963. As a Kennedy, he could have charmed his way to get those records from the administration, or obtained them covertly. Interestingly, his time at Phillips seems to correspond to the time when he began to form an obsession with who really killed his father. This was confirmed when Azzoni self-published a book in 2007 titled, *11 Letters and a Poem: John F. Kennedy, Jr., and Meg Azzoni.* In it, she writes that as a teenager in the late 1970s, JFK, Jr., was beginning to doubt the official version of events, and wanted to seek his own answers. "His heartfelt quest," she wrote, "was to expose and bring to trial who killed his father, and covered it up." Jeffries also said that he interviewed "another friend of JFK, Jr.'s, adult inner circle, who very adamantly requested to remain anonymous, verified that he was indeed quite knowledgeable about the assassination and often spoke of it in private."

Jeffries also claimed *George* was set to launch an investigation into the assassination in the very near future. This from his website (henrymakow.com): "Investigative reporter Wayne Madsen confirmed that he was scheduled to meet with JFK, Jr., the following week to discuss joining *George* magazine, where his primary focus would be investigating the assassination of President John F. Kennedy."

Which brings us to the strange story of a man named True Ott. Jeffries and Azonni provide ample evidence of Kennedy's desire to investigate the assassination. Therefore, I hesitate to undermine that conclusion in any way, but it is hard to ignore what this man had to say about the assassination of President Kennedy, and his own connection to John F. Kennedy, Jr. Essentially, Ott claims that he came into possession of clear evidence of the involvement of George H. W. Bush in the Kennedy assassination, and handed this over to JFK, Jr., just before Kennedy's plane crash. He made this known to JFK assassination expert John Hankey in a series of emails he exchanged with Hankey in June 2007. On September 12, 2007, Hankey published an article on rense.com to reveal what Ott had told him. To his credit, Hankey was quite skeptical of Ott and this story, which is reflected in the questions he asks Ott throughout their email exchanges.

"I've been engaging in an email correspondence with a health food store owner in Utah named True Ott, regarding John Kennedy Jr.'s final days. Ott says that John Jr. was murdered because he had come into possession, through Ott, of thorough and conclusive proof of George Bush Sr.'s direct involvement in the assassination of JFK. Ott says John was preparing to publish the information. The story Ott tells is incredible, and I certainly did not believe it the first time I heard it," said Hankey. "However,.. I've investigated and found that Ott is well known and respected nationally in the health food community. Ott is also listed on the Sierra Club and NRDC websites for the activism he claims brought him to the attention of *George* magazine." One has to wonder what Ott would gain from spreading this story if it was not true. Many involved in the JFK assassination have met mysterious deaths. "He has an important reputation as a respected environmental and health activist that is not helped by spreading ridiculous stories; and he assures me he wouldn't jeopardize his reputation like this if the story weren't true," said Hankey.

Here is an excerpt from their email exchange, publicly available on rense.com

True Ott writes as follows:

John:

I will never forget the phone call on the 4th of July weekend, 1999 - the phone call from John Jr. thanking me profusely for the information and the file. When he told me that a grand jury was to be convened and Bush was going to be indicted for the murder of his father, I tell you, I had goose bumps. For your review, here is an excerpt of what I wrote 3 years ago in my unpublished manuscript "Free at Last" concerning the event...

In addition to the murder of John Sr., keep in mind the file also contained evidence concerning C.I.A. orders for contract murders for witnesses of the event. There were over ten "collateral assassinations", one of which was the Dallas PD detective that was the focus of the DVD I sent you (Two Men in Dallas). Did you get that ok...

In answer to your question – it was about a week after John's plane went down. I had received about 8 calls from major news publications, (U.S. News and World Report, Time, Wall Street Journal, etc.) asking about reports that I had provided a file to John – "Did I, and what did the file contain?" I denied all, and made no comment. It was at this time that George Magazine called me as well – I think it was the editor Richard, though I am not completely certain. He told me the story was "dead" and the magazine was folding. He also told me that all evidence went with John – and that their offices had been burgled. You are right of course, it doesn't make sense that there were not any backup files– apparently they were taken as well. Again, this was a time of EXTREME CONCERN for me and my family – and I don't remember a lot of the specific details clearly. I don't mind telling you that I indeed feared for my life for at least a month. Please understand that I don't believe I am paranoid – but when one verifies that ones phones have indeed been tapped, it makes one a bit concerned...

The "Las Vegas" Files are Examined In 1995, I was going through my safe and file cabinets, and came across the sealed, manila envelope that had been placed in my trust by my financial planning client a decade earlier. I had completely forgotten about it. I called his home to see what he wanted me to do with it. His wife informed me that Mr. C. had suffered a stroke a year earlier, and was confined to a nursing home. He was in his 70's now, and was not doing very well.

In short, she didn't know anything about the "file" and suggested that I could just dispose of it.

I tossed it into the trash bin, but then thought that I should at least see what all the fuss was about. In many ways, I wish I had never opened it. It was a true "Pandora's Box", and I was shocked to read its contents. It was "file #5" of a group of 7 files called the "Gemstone" files. I don't know what the other six files contained, but this one was a literal ball-buster. It was the FULL STORY of the C.I.A.-planned and executed contract "hit" of John Fitzgerald Kennedy, president of the United States. It was full of very complete specifics, including such things as photostats of cancelled checks, travel vouchers, orders on C.I.A. letterhead, personnel "lists" of participants, disposition of witnesses and evidence, etc. The problem was, I recognized the names of many of the key men who participated in the assassination, as well as the massive cover-up that followed.

These were not all Jewish organized crime bosses, some were men linked to my LDS church authorities and some were nationally prominent politicians in my beloved Republican Party! The file was extremely damning towards George HW Bush, who in 1963 was the C.I.A. head in Dallas. The obvious involvement of the F.B.I. and Dallas PD, and their subsequent squelching of information as outlined in the file made me physically sick. There was no person in Federal Law Enforcement that I could trust with this information, that is, IF IT WAS INDEED LEGITIMATE! At first, I refused to believe it could be legitimate at all. My paradigm of perception refused to believe it could possibly be factual. However, I could not understand WHY my "client" would have such a file, and WHY would he want it sent to Beverly Hills CA, as well as a notice sent to Hank Greenspan of the Las Vegas Sun newspaper, if my client happened to "die suspiciously"? Like I said, it was a definite "pandora's box", one that I soon realized was too big for me. I kept thinking I ought to shred its contents, but I couldn't bring myself to do so.

During the summer of 1998, I was involved in actively protesting the expansion of Circle 4 Farm's gigantic hog factory farm into Iron County. My grass-roots citizen's organization CRSA (Citizens for Responsible and Sustainable Agriculture) had received a bit of national notoriety, with a number of AP wire stories circulating the nation. One such story caught the eye of a publication called George Magazine. The editor and staff contacted me and scheduled an appointment to meet and review my story.

The editor of George Magazine flew into Cedar City in his private plane to meet me, and shoot a photo spread. We spent the entire day, a Saturday, together. At the end of the day, at a local steak house, we sat down for a concluding meal.

Over salad, I had to confess to the editor that I had never even heard of, much less read a copy of George Magazine until he had called me. He reached into his briefcase and produced a copy. Looking at it, I was surprised to see that it was owned and founded by John Kennedy Jr.

I asked him about "John, and his politics." I was told that John was a real "champion of the under-dog" and that was why they were producing the story on CRSA and me.

I commented: "I believe that my image of John is like most Americans. The enduring image of little 'John-John' courageously stepping forward and giving his best salute as the caisson carrying his father's body slowly rolled by. Tell me, does John accept the 'official Warren Commission' account of the assassination, or does he think there was more to it? At this late date, does it even matter?"

The editor nodded and said: "Of course he doesn't accept the Warren Commission, but there is not a lot he, or anyone else can do about it! And I guarantee you, it DOES INDEED matter, at least to him. It is one of his major goals in life to find out the Truth!"

I replied: "Has he ever heard of something called the 'Gemstone Files'?" With that, the air became electrified. The editor laid down his salad fork and said: "What do YOU know about the 'Gemstone'?"

"Oh, it just might be that I have a copy of file #5. Does that interest you?" I casually volunteered. "You can't be serious! Are you serious? Don't kid about something like that! Where did you get it?" he almost screamed.

The dinner was immediately over, even though our steaks were just coming in from the kitchen. We had them placed into containers to take with us. The editor had to SEE the infamous Gemstone immediately. He couldn't wait until the meal was finished.

It was late on a Saturday night in Cedar City, Utah. I handed him the file, and he offered to compensate me for it. I refused. I asked him only one thing in return; if the information proved out to be genuine, that I needed to know. I just wanted justice to be served, and the guilty parties prosecuted.

I was awakened the next morning at 5:00. John's editor explained that he had been up all night reading the file. He had called John directly, and he was told to fly it immediately back to John. John had again offered to compensate me up to $10,000 for the lead. He felt it was that good. I politely refused, and gently reminded him of my earlier request. I just wanted to know if the information was genuine. To me, that would be payment enough.

The rest of 1998 went by quickly. The national political stage was being set. It looked like George W. Bush was seeking to secure the nomination to run against Al Gore.

On the 5th of July, 1999, my home phone rang. Joan answered it and said: "True, it's for you." As I answered it, a very polite masculine voice on the other end said: "Hello, True Ott, do you have a moment to speak? This is John Kennedy calling!"

I immediately asked him to hold while I went to the privacy of my home office to take his call. After a few minutes of small talk, he told me: "Well, I understand that you want to know what I think of your file. I want you to know that I have spent over six figures in private investigators to verify its contents. I can say to you without hesitation that its contents are indeed factual. As a matter of fact, because of this file, a federal grand jury will be convening within the next few weeks. It is my opinion, as well as my attorneys, that this federal grand jury will pass down an indictment against George Herbert Walker Bush for conspiracy to commit murder against my father, and will also indict others as the evidence unfolds. If George W. thinks he can run for dogcatcher after this grand jury convenes and his father indicted, he is sorely mistaken."

I was thrilled, yet deeply saddened by John's disclosures to me. I asked him how he felt about what he was about to do. Did he understand that it would shake American politics, especially the Republican Party to its very foundation?

He replied: "Yes, I do realize the gravity of the story and my accusations, but the guilty must be brought to justice."

I pressed: "But Mr. Kennedy, how do YOU feel?"

The phone went silent for a minute or two. Then John replied: "I feel like a mighty weight has been lifted from my shoulders. For the first time in my life, I feel empowered. I feel my Father's spirit beside me on this, and finally, I can exorcise a few demons from my life." He was definitely emotional, and very close to tears. I knew that I was. I was a part of American history. I had helped a brother's search for truth.

I warned him to be careful, that such actions were potentially very dangerous. He agreed, and said that he was "taking every precaution."

Then, in a quiet voice, he asked me for my banking information. He wished to wire $50K to my account. I told him thanks, but no thanks. "Give it to charity," I said, "I don't think it right to accept money for such terrible information. I am totally satisfied knowing that the file went to the very person that needed it the very most! Above all, John, please BE CAREFUL!"

John Kennedy Jr. thanked me profusely, and said that he wished there were more people in America like True Ott. He said that some day, he would somehow return the favor. I liked that. It was good to have made a friend such as John Kennedy.

A little over two weeks later, on July 16, 1999, John Kennedy Jr., along with his wife and her sister, were killed in a plane crash en route to Hyannisport for a family wedding. My new friend was gone, and the guilty involved in BOTH murders have still not been punished. I know the truth, however. There is no doubt whatsoever, why John was killed. It was NOT an accident!

Hankey then exchanged more emails with Ott, further trying to examine additional details in the story. There is no need to rehash all of that here, but other people have raised concerns about Ott as well, that his products do not work well, and that his biography is made up of accomplishments that cannot be independently verified. That is why I hesitated to bring him into this narrative. Hankey though seems to be satisfied that he is telling the truth, bringing up the old axiom that why do prostitutes have to have bad eyesight if they are testifying in court. Jim Garrison faced the same difficulty in his case against Clay Shaw, often having to rely on witnesses who were drug addicts or male prostitutes, which damaged their credibility. Maybe Ott does not make the highest quality health products, but that does not have to lead us to conclude that he is lying. Either way, even if JFK, Jr., had no interest in exposing the truth behind his father's assassination, the C.I.A. and the Bush family would still want to eliminate him anyway for two reasons. First, as we explored earlier, to clear the path to the White House for George W. Bush. The second would be continued intergenerational anger directed towards the Kennedy family on the part of the C.I.A. The agency killed both JFK and his brother Robert Kennedy. So therefore, we can put the JFK, Jr., assassination into context in terms of a final act of revenge on this family from the agency, many years in the making.

## The C.I.A. vs. The Kennedys

The assassination of John F. Kennedy, Jr., should also be viewed in the prism of a lasting hatred that the C.I.A. has harbored towards the Kennedy family for decades. His death then would just be the latest example of how this agency consistently undermined and eventually eliminated JFK, RFK, and even twice targeted Edward Kennedy as we will explore as well. For a full explanation of the C.I.A. motives for the Kennedy assassination, look no further than my book *Why the C.I.A. Killed JFK and Malcolm X: The Secret Drug Trade in Laos*. The rift between Kennedy and the agency began with the Bay of Pigs Invasion, which as we mentioned was in part organized by George H. W. Bush. The effort to depose Cuban dictator Fidel Castro completely failed. During the C.I.A.-backed invasion, the agency asked Kennedy to provide air support for the invaders, or stage a mass invasion. The president refused to do so, fearing the political fallout from attacking an unprovoked enemy, as well as a retaliatory response from the Soviet Union. Nevertheless, the agency felt the president could not be trusted to back their covert operations, and viewed him as soft on communism. Privately, the president felt the agency was deliberately trying to provoke him into starting a wider war with the Russians. Kennedy eventually fired C.I.A. Director Allen Dulles, and C.I.A. Director of Operations Richard Bissell. The agency responded by infiltrating JFK's pet program, the Peace Corps. Agents were pretending to be college students, and then joined the Peace Corps to go oversees to promote war. To this very day, if you were ever in the C.I.A. you cannot join the Peace Corps. After this the president became so angry with the agency that he told an administration official that he was "going to shatter the C.I.A. into a thousand pieces."

The following summer, the president did just that, issuing National Security Action Memorandums 55, 56, and 57. These directives shifted covert operations from the C.I.A. to the Joint Chiefs of Staff, and to the Department of Defense. Here is what NSAM 55 said:

a. I regard the Joint Chiefs of Staff as my principal military advisor responsible both for initiating advice to me and for responding to requests for advice. I expect their advice to come to me direct and unfiltered.

b. The Joint Chiefs of Staff have a responsibility for the defense of the nation in the Cold War similar to that which they have in conventional hostilities. They should know the military and paramilitary forces and resources available to the Department of Defense, verify their readiness, report on their accuracy, and make appropriate recommendations for their expansion and improvement. I look to the Chiefs to contribute dynamic and imaginative leadership in contributing to the success of the military and paramilitary aspects of Cold War programs.

The Chiefs would now be the "principal military advisor," not the C.I.A., and their advice must be "direct and unfiltered," implying that the agency had lied to him, and hid information. JFK would now be counting on the Chiefs' leadership in "paramilitary" operations, an area that had been assigned to the agency. As I said in my book, "This World War Two veteran was seeking to reestablish the model of 'conventional' warfare that worked during World War Two when there was no C.I.A., and the president and the Chiefs operated in tandem. NSAM 55 was a severe blow to the power, influence, and role of the Central Intelligence Agency. So was NSAM 57, issued that same day." It read in part:

> Any proposed paramilitary operation in the concept state will be presented to the Strategic Resources Group for initial consideration and for approval as necessary by the President. Thereafter, the SRG will assign primary responsibility for planning, for interdepartmental coordination and for execution to the task force, department or individual best qualified to carry forward the operation to success, and will indicate supporting responsibilities. Under this principle, the Department of Defense will normally receive responsibility for overt paramilitary operations. Where such an operation is to be wholly covert or disavowable, it may be assigned to C.I.A., provided that it is within the normal capabilities of the agency. Any large paramilitary operation wholly or partly covert which requires significant numbers of military trained personnel, amounts to military equipment which exceed normal C.I.A.-controlled stocks and/or military experience of a kind and level peculiar to the Armed services is properly the primary responsibility of the Department of Defense with the C.I.A. in a supporting role.

The president's policy in Laos is further examined in my book as a primary motivating factor to assassinate the president. Put simply, Laos is the best place on earth to grow opium. Since the 1950s the C.I.A. used the cover story of fighting communism in Southeast Asia to provide themselves easy access to the drug trade. The agency would use Air America planes to transport the opium and later convert it to heroin to sell to American GI's in Vietnam. The agency and the Joint Chiefs consistently pressured the president to commit 60,000 ground troops to Southeast Asia which he resisted at every turn. A massive commitment would mean years of access to the drug trade and a susceptible customer base to sell heroin to. On July 23, 1962, a Declaration of Neutrality for Laos was signed in Geneva which ordered the C.I.A. to leave Laos. It was not long before the agency began to retaliate. On August 5, 1962, less than two weeks after the Laotian peace accords, Marylin Monroe was found dead in her apartment. Instead of following the president's orders, the agents defied this order, and brought war back to Laos. They assassinated leaders loyal to JFK, all to get him to commit ground forces to win the civil war there. Richard Nixon recounted in his memoirs a revealing conversation that he had with Kennedy on April 20, 1961, one day after the Bay of Pigs Invasion failed. "I just don't think we ought to get involved, particularly where we might find ourselves fighting millions of Chinese troops in the jungles," Kennedy said. "In any event, I don't see how we can make a move in Laos, which is thousands of miles away, if we don't make a move in Cuba, which is only ninety miles away."

Kennedy felt the same way about Vietnam. The Sec Def Conference of May 1963, and another meeting of key JFK advisors in Hawaii in November 1963, both recommended a phased "Vietnamization" withdrawal from Vietnam by 1965. To this effect, JFK signed National Security Action Memorandum 263 on October 11, 1963, to recall the first 1,000 advisors of the 16,500 by December 1963. By November 1963 it was clear this president was not interested in any large-scale commitment to war in Southeast Asia which would spell an end to any hope for continued access to the drug trade. Not only that, there was a very good chance there was going to be four more years of JFK, considering his approval ratings, and polling done at the time against eventual nominee Barry Goldwater. A mock up poll conducted in March 1963 of JFK against Goldwater had Kennedy trouncing him 67% to 27%. A second term could not be tolerated by this rogue agency.

Proving the C.I.A.'s involvement in the Kennedy assassination is not even all that difficult any longer thanks to the work of many gifted historians, researchers, and investigators such as Jim Marrs, and New Orleans District Attorney Jim Garrison. Most importantly though are the recent revelations of longtime C.I.A. agent E. Howard Hunt. Before Hunt passed away in 2007, he offered a deathbed confession to his son St. John that detailed C.I.A. involvement in the Kennedy assassination. Four months after Hunt died, *Rolling Stone* did an article explaining nearly every detail of Hunt's deathbed confession regarding the JFK assassination. Much of what he said had been suspected by assassination researchers for years. Taken from my book, *Why the C.I.A. Killed JFK and Malcom X*, here are the six key men Hunt identified for the plot to kill the president:

C.I.A. Agent David Morales. Died in 1978 before he could be questioned by the House Select Committee on Assassinations. Like Hunt, he worked on the Bay Pigs Invasion fiasco, and blamed Kennedy for its failure. Recruited French assassin Lucien Sarti to be the sniper on the so-called "grassy knoll" to deliver the kill shot. Importantly Morales is a link to the southeast Asian drug trade, having served the agency both in Laos and Vietnam. He later bragged to a friend about the assassination saying, "We took care of that son of a bitch, didn't we?" This man took a lot of secrets to his grave.

C.I.A. Agent Frank Sturgis. Worked with Hunt and other

agents in covert operations in Cuba and Watergate, saying the break-in at Democratic headquarters in June 1972 was part of the cover-up of the JFK assassination. He also served as a link between the Mafia and the agency. Like Hunt, he was likely in Dallas on the day of the assassination, captured by the Dallas Morning News as one of the three "tramps."

Antonio Veciana. C.I.A. contract agent who failed in his attempt to kill Castro. Testified in front of Congress that he saw his C.I.A. contact, David Atlee Phillips, traveling with Lee Harvey Oswald in Dallas in the summer of 1963.

C.I.A. Agent David Atlee Phillips. Involved with Hunt and Sturgis in the failed Bay of Pigs Invasion. Phillips was the Mexico City C.I.A. Station Chief when it was visited by Oswald, who he was later seen with in September 1963 in Dallas. Recruited Veciana and Agent William K. Harvey into the plot. Went on to become C.I.A. operations chief in Latin America where he helped to organize a successful assassination plot against a Chilean politician in 1970.

C.I.A. Agent William K. Harvey. Longtime leader of clandestine operations and yet another link between the C.I.A. and the Mafia. In 1960, he was selected to lead a covert C.I.A. assassination team named ZR-RIFLE. He harbored bitter resentment toward JFK for his policies of peace, such as not invading Cuba, and for being demoted. Died in 1976 before he could testify in front of the House.

C.I.A. Agent Cord Meyer. In charge of "Operation Mockingbird," the C.I.A. domestic propaganda program that among other goals pushed the myth of the Domino Theory on the public. Mockingbird enlisted domestic and foreign journalists to push the C.I.A. agenda both at home and abroad through misinformation and infiltration of various groups... The selling of the Domino Theory, beginning in the 1950s by the C.I.A., was key to convincing the public to support various covert operations throughout the world, especially in Southeast Asia. His former wife, Mary, was a mistress of JFK. She was mysteriously killed in 1964. Cord Meyer was likely the group leader, coordinating the plot.

Another simple way to tie the agency to the John F. Kennedy assassination was provided by Jim Marrs in his book, *Crossfire*. The Mannlicher-Carcano rifle used to frame Lee Harvey Oswald for the assassination had ammunition that could be traced back to the C.I.A.

According to an F.B.I. document, the 6.5 mm ammunition found in the Texas School Book Depository was part of a batch manufactured on a U.S. government contract by Westin Cartridge Corporation of East Alton, Illinois, which is now a part of Winchester-Western Division of Olin Industries. In the mid-1950s the Marine Corps purchased four million rounds of this ammunition, prompting the author of one F.B.I. document to state, "The interesting thing about this order is that it is for ammunition which does not fit, and cannot be fired in any of the United States Marine Corps weapons. This gives rise to the obvious speculation that it is a contract for ammunition placed by the C.I.A. with Western Cartridge Corporation under a USMC cover for concealment purposes." It is well known that the C.I.A. used "sanitized" weapons – that is, weapons that cannot be traced directly back to the agency.

## Targeting Teddy

It was not just JFK that the agency targeted for assassination. Let us deal with Edward Kennedy as well. On June 19, 1964, Edward Kennedy nearly died in a mysterious plane crash. The Senate had just passed the Civil Rights Act, with Kennedy casting one of the decisive votes. This was just seven months after the Kennedy assassination, and one year after JFK proposed on national television the idea of a Civil Rights Act. For those who hated the Kennedys, this was a bad day, seeing the fulfillment of a key part of JFK's civil rights legacy. On the fiftieth anniversary of the plane crash, *Boston Magazine* summarized the salient facts.

Kennedy was 32 years-old, two years into the term he won in a special election. He was running late on his way to Springfield, Massachusetts, to accept the nomination for a full term in the Senate at the state Democratic Convention. Joining him were the convention's keynote speaker Senator Birch Bayh of Indiana, Bayh's wife Marvella, his legislative aide Edward Moss, and a pilot, Edwin Zimny. The group never made it to Springfield. Three miles from the runway, the plane flew too low, hit some trees, and crashed in an orchard. Moss and Zimny did not survive. The Bayhs escaped serious injury, and after helping his wife from the plane, Senator Bayh returned to pull Kennedy from the wreckage. Kennedy was alive, but in bad shape. He had broken three vertebrae and two ribs, and had a collapsed lung. The crash instantly became one more instance of the Kennedy family's bad luck. Ted's older brother and sister had both died in plane crashes.

One unusual aspect to this plane crash is that this charter plane was scheduled to leave much earlier in the day, when visibility would have been much better. A crash would have been avoided. The plane crashed in heavy fog at 11 p.m. EST. The two senators had been delayed from leaving the capital by a filibuster. Was the C.I.A. powerful enough to delay voting long enough in the Senate to force the Kennedy plane to travel in such dangerous conditions? Bayh had been elected to the Senate in 1962 and had been a key Kennedy supporter from the beginning of his term. Just like with the JFK, Jr., plane crash there were many people on board this plane that the agency would have liked to see dead. With JFK, Jr., it was him and his (perhaps pregnant) wife, thus taking out that family. Here both Edward Kennedy and Bayh would be assassinated. The agency may have been stewing over the fact that Bayh had beaten Homer E. Capehart for the Senate in 1962. Capehart had been a big supporter of the C.I.A., and perhaps the most vocal opponent of President Kennedy in the Senate. He spoke out against the Peace Corps, and advocated for the bombing or invasion of Cuba during the Cuban Missile Crisis, just like the C.I.A. had wanted, to avenge for the embarrassment of the Bay of Pigs Invasion. There is no doubt the agency would have had the motive, the means, and the opportunity to take down this plane.

It is amazing that these men survived. The fact that two died in the crash shows just how near they came to death. Kennedy came very close to death himself. He was taken to nearby Cooley Dickinson Hospital, where rescue workers frantically worked to revive him because he had no pulse, and his blood pressure was almost nonexistent," according to his press secretary Edward Martin. The staff "took heroic measures including blood transfusions in a successful attempt to rally the failing senator and the efforts paid off," Martin said, referring to the three units of blood and glucose that Kennedy was transfused with. A team of army doctors was later flown in from Walter Reed Army Medical Center in Washington. They were led by Brig. Gen. Henry S. Murphey who later credited Doctor Thomas Corriden, the hospital's chief of staff, with saving Kennedy's life.

We should note that the pilot, Edwin Zimny was hardly an inexperienced pilot, who would be unfamiliar with bad conditions, or take risks with his passengers. He was the owner and operator of Zimny's Flying Service in Lawrence, Massachusetts. At 48 years-old he had years of flying under his belt, both alone and as a commercial instructor and mechanic. Pilot error was judged to be the cause of the crash. Was there any explosion on the aircraft? Later, Kennedy recalled to a reporter something unusual. "My first thought," he said, "was that the plane had been hit by lightning. I saw black things outside my window. I could see car lights, but the plane then began a steep climb." So, this "lightning" happened before the plane crashed. Also notice that Kennedy said the plane began a steep climb, not a descent. Does this prove that the pilot saw the mountains ahead, but was unable to fly the airplane high enough because there was an explosion that disabled part of the aircraft?

The plane was lent to the senators by businessman Daniel E. Hogan, also from Lawrence,

Massachusetts. Zimny had used the plane before to bring Kennedy back and forth from Boston to Washington, so he was hardly unfamiliar with the hill he crashed into, having taken the same route before. Perhaps the addition of Bayh being on the flight this time was just too irresistible for the C.I.A. Who exactly was Daniel E. Hogan? The answer comes to us in the book, *Spy Capitalism: Itek and the C.I.A.*, written by Jonathan E. Lewis. In this book, he details that Itek was a front company for the C.I.A., doing work in some cases for Boston University and business with The First National Bank of Boston. Lawrence, Massachusetts, by the way, is less than an hour drive from Boston. Lewis reports in the endnotes that one of the members of the board of directors was the same Daniel E. Hogan, making this plane easily accessible to the C.I.A.

And then there is Chappaquiddick. Here is the official version of events accepted by history.com.

Shortly after leaving a party on Chappaquiddick Island, Senator Edward "Ted" Kennedy of Massachusetts drives an Oldsmobile off a wooden bridge into a tide-swept pond. Kennedy escaped the submerged car, but his passenger, 28-year-old Mary Jo Kopechne, did not. The senator did not report the fatal car accident for 10 hours. On the evening of July 18, 1969... Kennedy and his cousin Joe Gargan were hosting a cookout and party at a rented cottage on Chappaquiddick Island, an affluent island near Martha's Vineyard, Massachusetts. The party was planned as a reunion for Kopechne and five other women, all veterans of the late Senator Robert F. Kennedy's 1968 presidential campaign... Just after 11 p.m., Kennedy left the party with Kopechne, by his account to drive to the ferry slip where they would catch a boat back to their respective lodgings in Edgartown on Martha's Vineyard. While driving down the main roadway, Kennedy took a sharp turn onto the unpaved Dike Road, drove for a short distance, and then missed the ramp to a narrow wooden bridge and drove into Poucha Pond. Kennedy, a married man, claimed the Dike Road excursion was a wrong turn. However, both he and Kopechne had previously driven down the same road, which led to a secluded ocean beach just beyond the bridge.

However, this does not seem to be close to the truth. Consider these quotes recorded in the Oval Office on March 13, 1973, by President Richard Nixon. He was speaking to White House Counsel John Dean.

Dean...if they get those bank records between the start of July of 1969 through June of 1971...there comes Chappaquiddick with a vengeance...

Nixon: (unintelligible)

Dean...if they get to it...that is going to come out, and this whole thing can turn around on that. If Kennedy knew what a bear trap he was walking into...

Assassination expert R. B. Cutler in the book *The Conspiracy*

*Reader*, convincingly portrays this event much differently. In Cutler's view, this was a C.I.A.-orchestrated political assassination to remove any chance of Edward Kennedy running for president in 1972. This type of hit "did not necessitate killing him. In fact, a third shooting would have been poorly advised, perhaps awakening the country to the obvious fact that the agency was killing the Kennedys. No better bear trap could have been set than an engineered automobile accident that involved 'booze, blondes, and the beach.'" The scandal of this "C.I.A.-orchestrated ambush left him politically dead. Forced to lie about being behind the wheel, Kennedy dropped out of the presidential campaign nine months later." Cutler asks, "With C.I.A. guns at your back, how deliberate were your mysterious hints like... whether the girl might still be alive somewhere out of the immediate area?"

Cutler's evidence, based off years of interviews and research is compelling. The skid marks on the bridge where Kennedy allegedly drove off go straight. They do not turn even one degree towards the direction the car went off the bridge, indicating they were put there at a different time. The speed of the car at the time of the "accident" is also an issue. Kennedy claimed, as did the Registry of Motor Vehicles, that the Oldsmobile was travelling 22 miles an hour. Cutler determined that skid marks are impossible to produce at such a slow speed, as well as flying 36 feet into the water. The author, along with the help of an engineer, determined the car would have to be traveling at least 40 miles an hour when it flew off the bridge to travel 36 feet in the air.

Cutler also points out that according to her friends, Kopechne had nothing alcoholic to drink at the party. Yet, the coroner's report said that she had .10 blood alcohol level. That suggests she was injected with alcohol, or forced to drink it against her will. In fact, evidence supports that she was injected with something because according to Cutler, on her blouse, "around the collar, almost all the way down the back, and on both sleeves, a very large area, residual traces of blood were found in testing about three weeks after the accident." The author tried to confirm this with the coroner's office in Boston. He told the coroner that he wanted to make a drawing of where the blood was. The man told Cutler he would help, but to call back next week. When the author did, the coroner changed his mind and said he wanted nothing to do with him.

Cutler constructed a scenario where a car of five C.I.A. agents stops Kennedy. Then they drug him, or knock him unconscious to take him across the ferry to the Shiretown Inn. He wakes up the next morning, chats with some friends, and only then finds out Mary Jo was dead. This makes better sense than the ridiculous claim that he swam a mile to the inn, while supposedly intoxicated and exhausted from trying to save Mary Jo. In reality, she had been taken by two agents, drugged and sent to her watery death in Kennedy's car. The official timeline also does not make sense. The accident allegedly occurred around 11 p.m. However, Deputy Sheriff Huck Look spotted the Kennedy car on dry land at 12:45 a.m. with two passengers in front, and a slumped dark shape in the back. Cutler also points out that Kennedy was never actually spotted asking for help, only someone who stood in the shadows and called for assistance. This person may have even used a voice box (Cutler suggests the involvement of E. Howard Hunt here) to impersonate the senator, because by then the real Kennedy was across the water.

Cutler summed up the analysis by noting that "they have a whole bunch of people in the C.I.A. who've been doing this sort of thing all over the world. All they do is sit around and figure out how to pull it off. And they have a wonderful time," the author said. "I still maintain they had a boat; a small outboard was seen at about two-thirty by a few witnesses. There are so many details. The information is there."

## RFK's Obsession

Having now dealt with Edward Kennedy, let us move on to the Robert Kennedy assassination. Again, just to reemphasize the point we are making here, the idea that the C.I.A. would assassinate John F. Kennedy, Jr., makes sense in the context of the agency having targeted all three of his surviving uncles. The parallel is especially relevant though when it comes to Robert Kennedy. JFK, Jr., and RFK shared an important motive when it came to why the agency wanted to kill both men, namely their shared desire to prove that the C.I.A. killed President Kennedy. If the agency, at least in part killed RFK to help conceal the truth, it makes sense they would do the same with JFK, Jr.

As attorney general, Robert Kennedy was making inquiries into the assassination from the moment of the murder. On November 22, 1963, RFK confronted C.I.A. Director John McCone, and asked him directly if the C.I.A. planned the assassination. RFK was a lawyer, and a relentless researcher with a tenacious personality. He concluded after several years of investigation that the C.I.A. had killed his brother. He met with conspiracy researchers Penn Jones, Jr., and Walter Sheridan to seek out information on the assassination. He also made a private trip to the C.I.A. station in Mexico City where Oswald allegedly visited before the assassination. Kennedy believed that the only way for the truth to be revealed would be for him to use the powers of the presidency to open a new investigation, and bring justice to those who killed JFK. If this happened, it would likely bring an end to the agency, with several of the planners executed for treason. The definition of treason is "the crime of betraying one's country, especially by attempting to kill the sovereign or overthrow the government." RFK also made it clear several times during his campaign for president in 1968 that if elected he would bring an immediate end to the Vietnam War. He even said this directly when he was giving his final speech after winning the California primary. This would spell an end to the burgeoning drug trade in Laos and Vietnam. RFK therefore was a major threat to the wealth, power, and existence of this rogue agency. He had to be eliminated.

Surprisingly, it is not even all that difficult to prove the agency was behind this assassination. The reason is that the assassin himself has said as much. Just so we are clear, Senator Robert Kennedy died on June 6, 1968, after being shot in a kitchen pantry at the Ambassador Hotel Ballroom in downtown Los Angeles. He had just won the California primary, all but assuring him of the Democratic nomination for the presidency. The official version of events is that he was shot by one man, Sirhan Sirhan, who as of 2017 is still alive in a California prison. As I said in my book *Why the C.I.A. Killed JFK and Malcolm X*, it is clear the agency was behind this:

In February 2011, Sirhan's attorney, William Pepper made a dramatic announcement. He was seeking to either gain a new trial for Sirhan, or have him released on parole for two reasons. First, the assassin was hypnoprogrammed by the C.I.A. to commit the assassination, plus the shot that killed RFK could never have come from him. After years of hypnosis and examination by psychiatrists, Pepper said there was, "no doubt he does not remember the critical events. He is not feigning it. It's not an act. He does not remember it. It was very clear to me that this guy did not kill Bob Kennedy." Sirhan asserted to his lawyers that he was "brainwashed" to commit the murder so that he could be the patsy, and the true forces behind the assassination would never be known. His lack of memory of the event, his trance-like behavior on the day of the shooting, and his automatic writing exercises in his journal (where he would obsessively write "RFK must die") are some of the factors that indicate he was a member of the C.I.A.'s MKULTRA program that trained robotic-like assassins. Sirhan's other lawyer Lawrence Teeter said that

Sirhan was forced against his will to take part in this program that used drugs, chemicals, and sensory deprivation to control the will of the assassin, removing that person's culpability in the committing of the crime. The C.I.A. conducted these secret experimental programs in the 1950s and 1960s at the height of the Cold War. Not surprisingly, Sirhan's chance for a new trial, and for parole were both denied.

It is also clear that Sirhan was not the only gunman firing at RFK. Kennedy fundraiser Nina Rhodes-Hughes was standing just a few feet away from RFK when the shooting began. She insisted that she saw a different gunman firing at Kennedy, a man who was not Sirhan Sirhan. However, her statements to the authorities were altered against her will. "What has to come out is that there was another shooter to my right," Rhodes Hughes said in April 2012. "The truth has got to be told. No more cover-ups." She said that the F.B.I. changed her statement to make it look like she told them that there were only 8 shots. "I never said eight shots. I never, never said it," she said. "There were more than eight shots ... There were at least 12, maybe 14. And I know there were because I heard the rhythm in my head."

We also know that C.I.A. agents were spotted at the crime scene as well due to the work of BBC filmmaker Shane O'Sullivan. After a three-year investigation, he aired a documentary on the BBC's Newsnight program in November 2006. During the program, O'Sullivan positively identified C.I.A. agent David Morales as being at the Ambassador Hotel on the night of the assassination. O'Sullivan also identified fellow C.I.A. agents Gordon Campbell, and George Joannides as being there as well. The filmmaker reported that there was no reason these agents should have been in L.A. because they were based out of Southeast Asia. O'Sullivan included a quote from Morales who told his friends, "I was in Dallas when we got the son of a bitch, and I was in Los Angeles when we got the little bastard."

A larger point needs to be made here to understand the JFK, Jr., assassination in the context of these slayings. If you read my book, *Why the C.I.A. Killed JFK and Malcolm X,* and the work of many other historians, you can find out the history of how the agency executed both Malcolm X and Dr. Martin Luther King, Jr., as well. Collectively the agency through these four assassinations established their own rogue government, answerable to only themselves. Perhaps the last best chance to stop them died on June 6, 1968. Largely through their black budget from the Congress, and their endless supply of money garnered from access to the opium trade in Southeast Asia and Afghanistan, the agency can in effect do anything that they want, regardless of who the president happens to be at any moment in time. Therefore, President Clinton would have been powerless to stop this agency from killing John F. Kennedy, Jr.

In fact, killing JFK, Jr., during Clinton's administration would have an enormous appeal within the agency given Clinton's documented affinity for the Kennedys. Clinton would have loved the symmetry of the son of his political hero to succeed him in the White House and cement his legacy for the 21st Century. The assassination could be viewed as a final act of retribution against a president that the agency did not get along with. The list is long of examples of the tension between the C.I.A. and Clinton, who "fired" directors three separate times, giving him four C.I.A. directors for his two terms. In general, the agency did not like his containment policy with Iraq, where he steadfastly refused to deploy ground troops. Another point of contention with the agency was their increasing frustration with his unwillingness to target Osama bin Laden. *The Washington Post* ran this article on February 16, 2016: "Bill Clinton and the missed opportunities to kill Osama bin Laden." In it, reporter Glenn Kessler documented nine times the agency was told to stand down from trying to kill bin Laden by their commander-in-chief. The eighth chance seemed to be the best opportunity the agency had, according to the 9/11 commission report:

> It was in Kandahar that perhaps the last, and most likely the best, opportunity arose for targeting Bin Laden with cruise missiles before 9/11... CIA assets in Afghanistan reported on Bin Laden's location in and around Kandahar over the course of five days and nights. The reporting was very detailed and came from several sources. If this intelligence was not "actionable," working-level officials said at the time and today, it was hard for them to imagine how any intelligence on Bin Laden in Afghanistan would meet the standard. Communications were good, and the cruise missiles were ready. "This was in our strike zone," a senior military officer said. "It was a fat pitch, a home run." He expected the missiles to fly. When the decision came back that they should stand down, not shoot, the officer said, "we all just slumped." He told us he knew of no one at the Pentagon or the CIA who thought it was a bad gamble. Bin Laden "should have been a dead man" that night, he said.

This lost chance was in May 1999. Two months later, JFK, Jr., was dead. I am not ready to say that the Clinton presidency, his affection for the Kennedy's, and his tension with the C.I.A. was why JFK., Jr; was killed. I still believe Kennedy's threat to the Bush family, his willingness to expose the truth about the JFK assassination, and CIA hatred of the Kennedys, all tie in to the motives of why the agency killed him. However, I do not want to rule out the role the Clinton presidency may have played as an extra motivating factor to devastate not just one family, but two when that plane went down on July 16, 1999.

President Clinton offered these remarks to a stunned nation. "John Kennedy and his sister, and later his wife, were uncommonly kind to my daughter and to my wife," Clinton said during a press conference with Israeli Prime Minister Ehud Barak, on July 19, 1999. "This has been a very difficult thing for us personally."

After the JFK assassination, the creator of the C.I.A., President Harry Truman, began to express grave reservations about this agency. Jfkfacts.org offers an important look at how Truman could see the monster that he had created was getting out of control:

"For some time I have been disturbed by the way the CIA has been diverted from its original assignment," wrote former president Harry Truman in the *Washington Post* on December 22, 1963. It was exactly one month after the assassination of President Kennedy. "It has become an operational and at times a policy-making arm of the Government. This has led to trouble and may have compounded our difficulties in several explosive areas," Truman wrote. The former president never explicitly linked JFK's death to the clandestine service, but the timing and venue of his piece was suggestive. Already Soviet bloc news outlets were speculating Kennedy's murder – and the murder of the only suspect while in police custody – pointed to U.S. government involvement in the assassination. Truman addressed the allegations obliquely. "This quiet intelligence arm of the President has been so removed from its intended role that it is being interpreted as a symbol of sinister and mysterious foreign intrigue – and subject for cold war enemy propaganda," Truman wrote.

Truman said he knew the first two directors of the CIA and called them "men of the highest character, patriotism and integrity." He added he could only assume the same about "all those who continue in charge." But he had stiff words for the agency's leaders. He said the CIA's "operational duties" should "be terminated." In short, JFK's assassination prompted Truman to call for the CIA's abolition. There can be little doubt that the circumstances of Kennedy's murder prompted Truman's radical proposal. The former president, living in Missouri, began writing his *Post* article nine days after Kennedy was killed, according to an excellent 2009 piece by former CIA officer Ray McGovern (who says he was relying on JFK researcher Ray Marcus). In handwritten notes found at the Truman Library, the former president noted, among other things, that the CIA had worked as he intended only "when I had control." Four months later, former CIA director Allen Dulles paid Truman a visit. Dulles tried to get Truman to retract what he had written in the *Post*. "No dice, said Truman," according to McGovern/Marcus. But four days later, in a formal memo for Lawrence Houston, the CIA's general counsel, Dulles fabricated a retraction. He claimed that Truman told him the *Washington Post* article was "all wrong," and that Truman "seemed quite astounded at it." Truman denied it. In a June 10, 1964, letter to *Look* magazine, Truman restated his critique of covert action, emphasizing that he never intended the CIA to get involved in "strange activities."

## Why July 16?

I already mentioned earlier that the middle of July would be appropriate for the plotters to celebrate the assassination of John F. Kennedy, Jr., due to the time they could count on to spend in seclusion at the Bohemian Grove each year. However, there is more to that date than the connection to the Bohemian Grove.

When John F. Kennedy, Jr.'s, plane crashed on July 16, 1999, the tragedy was felt deeply within the Kennedy family. Also on the plane of course was his wife Carolyn, and her sister Lauren Bessette. At Martha's Vineyard, where the plane went down, Kennedy was going to drop off Bessette, and from there head to the Kennedy compound on Cape Cod's Hyannisport. The couple was going to attend the marriage of Rory Kennedy, the youngest child of Robert F. Kennedy. The whole weekend was set aside for the wedding and for the family and friends to enjoy each other's company, with most leaving on Sunday, July 18.

So why then? Is it just a coincidence that on this same weekend exactly 30 years prior there was another Kennedy family party that ended in disaster? July 18, 1969, was when the C.I.A. ambushed Edward Kennedy at Chappaquiddick. Both parties were centered around the late Robert Kennedy; the 1969 party to honor RFK campaign workers, and the 1999 party to celebrate RFK's youngest daughter getting married. We just noted above how much hatred the C.I.A. especially harbored towards "the little bastard" Robert Kennedy due to his plans to end the Vietnam War, and expose the truth of the JFK assassination. The C.I.A. probably planned for JFK, Jr.'s, body to be recovered on July 18, 1999, the 30th anniversary of Chappaquiddick, in some sadistic twist. The recovery of the wreckage was not a matter of national security, nor a military operation. Three civilians had died. Nevertheless, within hours the C.I.A. was sweeping the area with three KH-11 photographic satellites to find the bodies. In fact, the agency knew that Edward Kennedy would of course be at this wedding party for his niece in the same location as the Chappaquiddick ambush 30 years early. Perhaps the irony was just too much for them to pass up.

We can go back further with this date. We noted already how July 1962 was a bad month for the C.I.A. On July 23, 1962, a Declaration of Neutrality was signed for Laos, spelling a potential end to C.I.A. access to the opium market in Laos. Exactly one week before though, on July 16, 1962, the president did something else though that may have angered the agency even more deeply, on a personal level. Late on that Monday evening, Kennedy began an affair with the ex-wife of C.I.A. agent Cord Meyer. Her name was Mary Pinchot Meyer. Michael O'Brien in his book *John F. Kennedy: A Biography*, briefly discusses the beginning of the affair with Meyer, who was also the sister of *Washington Post* editor Ben

Bradlee's wife Tony. Allegedly, they smoked marijuana together that had been provided by *Washington Post* Executive Editor Jim Truitt. It is possible that the Kennedy-Meyer affair began years earlier in 1954 when the Kennedys and Meyers were neighbors in Washington, D.C. Was Kennedy playing with fire by re-igniting this former flame? Marylin Monroe's death just weeks later may be viewed in this light as well, as retaliation for JFK going after Mary Pinchot Meyer. Keep in mind that E. Howard Hunt said that Cord Meyer was one of the key men who helped plan the entire JFK assassination. Cord Meyer died on March 13, 2001, long enough to be around to witness the third Kennedy assassination. Bradlee confirmed that C.I.A. agent James Jesus Angleton confiscated Mary Pinchot Meyer's diary after she was shot execution-style while jogging in a Washington, D.C., park on October 12, 1964. A young black man was imprisoned for the crime, and later acquitted.

After July 16, 1999, a strange pattern of significant events began to happen to Governor George Bush and later President Bush, all on the anniversary of that fateful day. Let us begin with July 16, 2000, as Bush was preparing to announce to the world who his running mate would be. Bush met with Richard Cheney, and his key top advisors at the governor's mansion in Austin on July 15. By the following day Bush had made up his mind that Cheney would be his vice president. The mainstream media reflected this assumption in their reporting of the meeting the following day as well. By July 16, 2000, it was clear within Bush's inner circle, and within his own mind that Cheney would be his running mate.

July 16, 2001, was equally important as well. The president held a summit with Russian President Vladimir Putin, where he got a sense of his "soul." Also on July 16, of that year, British Intelligence shared a report warning that Al Qaeda was in the final stages of planning an attack on the west.

On the three-year anniversary of JFK, Jr.'s, plane crash,

President George W. Bush was making some news of his own. July 16, 2002, was an important day for the new president. In the aftermath of the 9/11 terrorist attacks, Bush proposed sweeping changes to give himself broad executive authority to wage war on terrorism, with a new Department of Homeland Security that would undermine the C.I.A. and report directly to him.

On July 16, 2003, C.I.A. Director George Tenet was falling on a sword for his commander-in-chief behind closed doors in the U.S. capitol. Tenet was explaining why Bush lied to the country in his State of the Union Address that Iraq possessed uranium to make weapons of mass destruction. "They have undermined America's prestige and credibility in the world," Senator Edward Kennedy said in a speech delivered at the Johns Hopkins School of Advanced International Studies. Michigan Sen. Carl Levin, the top Democrat on the Senate Armed Services Committee, agreed. "The misleading statement about African uranium is not an isolated issue," he said. Levin said Bush's statement was "one of several questionable statements and exaggerations" in the buildup to war. "It is therefore essential that we have a thorough, open and bipartisan inquiry into the objectivity, credibility and use of U.S. intelligence before the Iraq war," Levin said in a Senate floor speech. Perhaps it was these comments and others that drove Bush to continue the war for years to come.

On July 16, 2004, the administration announced support for a massive surge in military spending and construction, close to a four percent increase from the previous year.

July 16, 2005, was spent trying to persuade Congress in his weekly radio address to give a fair hearing to his as-yet unnamed nominee to the Supreme Court.

July 16, 2006, was another anniversary when the second term president was trying to project himself as a strong leader. He spent the day at the G8 Summit in St. Petersburg meeting with world leaders such as Putin, and Chinese President Hu Jintao.

July 16, 2007, continued the military theme conspicuously

found on this day, when President Bush met with President Ryszard Kaczynski, of the Republic of Poland. They discussed the importance of NATO, and having an effective missile defense shield for Eastern Europe.

For Bush's final July 16, the lame duck president saved the best for last, steadfastly refusing to put a timetable on withdrawing troops from Iraq. *The New York Times* reported "Mr. Bush also sought to rebut criticism from Senator Barack Obama of Illinois, the presumptive Democratic presidential nominee, who on Tuesday accused the administration of having a 'single-minded and open-ended focus' on Iraq. Mr. Bush disputed that the war in Iraq had distracted the administration from the resurgence of the Taliban and Al Qaeda in Afghanistan." On that day, Bush also made a stunning move to keep his vice president and perhaps himself away from an impeachment trial. *The New York Times* reported:

President Bush invoked executive privilege to keep Congress from seeing the F.B.I. report of an interview with Vice President Dick Cheney and other records related to the administration's leak of CIA operative Valerie Plame's identity in 2003. The president's decision drew a sharp protest Wednesday from Rep. Henry Waxman, chairman of House Oversight Committee, which had subpoenaed Attorney General Michael Mukasey to turn over the documents. "This unfounded assertion of executive privilege does not protect a principle; it protects a person," the California Democrat said. "If the vice president did nothing wrong, what is there to hide?" Waxman left little doubt he would soon move for a committee vote to hold Mukasey in contempt of Congress. Bush's assertion of privilege prevented Mukasey from complying with the House subpoena for records bearing on the unmasking of Plame at a time that the administration was trying to rebut criticism from her husband, former U.S.

Ambassador Joseph Wilson, of Bush's rationale for going to war in Iraq.

July 16 is a date that should live in infamy.

## Chapter Three

# The alleged Israeli motive

Another potential group of people who may have wanted to see Kennedy dead was the intelligence community within the Israeli government. One of these agencies is Shin Bet, which functions much like the F.B.I., and the United States Secret Service combined into one entity. Here is how BBC News profiled them three years after JFK, Jr.'s, death.

Shin Bet, also known as the General Security Services, or Shabak, is Israel's domestic security agency. It is believed to be at the forefront of undercover operations against Palestinian militants. The agency is said to run a network of Palestinian informers and to have a key role in the Israeli assassination policy against alleged militants.

Shin Bet is believed to have three operational wings:

Arab affairs department: Responsible for anti-terrorist operations related to alleged Palestinian and Arab terrorists. This department is believed to have an undercover detachment, popularly known as the Mista'arvim (Marauders) who work to counter the intifada.

Non-Arab affairs department: Formerly divided into communist and non-communist sections. Concerned with all other countries, including penetrating foreign intelligence services and diplomatic missions in Israel.

Protective security department: Responsible for protecting Israeli Government buildings and embassies, defense industries, scientific installations, industrial plants, and the national airline.

Shin Bet's reputation has suffered in recent years. It's reputation was further compromised by its failure to prevent the assassination of Israeli Prime Minister Yitzhak Rabin in 1995 by a right-wing Israeli extremist. The agency's head, Karmi Gillon, resigned as a result of the assassination.

The other intelligence agency within Israel is Mossad, a group like the C.I.A., that deals with foreign intelligence. The political science journal *Global Security* defines them like this:

Mossad [Hebrew for "institution"] has responsibility for human intelligence collection, covert action, and counterterrorism. Its focus is on Arab nations and organizations throughout the world. Mossad also is responsible for the clandestine movement of Jewish refugees out of Syria, Iran, and Ethiopia. Mossad agents are active in the former communist countries, in the West, and at the UN. Mossad is headquartered in Tel Aviv. The staff of Mossad was estimated during the late 1980s to number between 1,500 to 2,000 personnel, with more recent estimates placing the staff at an estimated 1,200 personnel. The identity of the director of Mossad was traditionally a state secret, or at least not widely publicized, but, in March 1996, the Government announced the appointment of Major General Danny Yatom as the replacement for Shabtai Shavit, who resigned in early 1996. Danny Yatom resigned on February 24, 1998, following the release of the Ciechanover Commission report which dealt with the failed attempt to assassinate Khalid Meshaal, a top Hamas political leader, and thus found faults with his performance as head of Mossad. Yatom was replaced in early March 1998 by Efraim Halevy, then Israel's representative to the European Union.

What does all of this have to do with the death of John F. Kennedy, Jr.? Potentially nothing, but in the spirit of leaving every avenue of research explored, let us find out what connections there may be.

Conspiracy author, editor, and publisher Kenn Thomas has done extensive research on the death of John F. Kennedy, Jr. He was interviewed for the program, "Encounters with the Unexplained." Here is a sample of his author profile found on Amazon.com.

Kenn Thomas works as a conspiracy writer, a parapolitical researcher, university library archivist, and showrunner for Steamshovel Press, a parapolitical conspiracy cyber presence and magazine. He has written books on the Inslaw affair, co-authoring *The Octopus* with the late Jim Keith, and on Fred Crisman and the Maury Island Incident. Thomas has authored over a dozen books on various conspiracy topics. The latest is *JFK & UFO*, about the possibility that 1947 UFO witness Fred Crisman was connected to the assassination of John F. Kennedy; and *The Octopus: Secret Government and the Death of Danny Casolaro*, about the Inslaw affair. In 2004, Feral House published a new edition of *The Octopus*, extending the suggestion of connections to the post-9/11 world and al-Qaeda. Feral House also recently published the new book, fully titled *JFK & UFO: Military-Industrial Conspiracy and Cover-Up from Maury Island to Dallas*. Thomas calls his research interest "parapolitics," the study of conspiracies of all colors – from alien abductions and the Illuminati, to the John F. Kennedy assassination and the September 11, 2001 attacks. *The New Yorker* called his work "on the cutting edge" of conspiracy.

Thomas believes that there might have been a motive on the part of these agencies to want to kill Kennedy. "In the months preceding his death, Kennedy's magazine ran an article about the assassination of Yitzhak Rabin, the Israeli prime minister. The article implies that Rabin was the victim of a conspiracy, and that the lone gunman who was convicted of the crime was simply a patsy." The article in question ran in the March 1997 edition of *George*. It was written by the mother of the accused assassin, and specifically implicated people within the Shin Bet as being directly involved with the assassination, or suspiciously negligent in their protection of the prime minister.

Therefore, the motive would be one of revenge against Kennedy, if the Shin Bet were indeed somehow involved in Kennedy's death. If the motive was revenge, this is a motive based off human emotions that tend to be acted out soon after the wronged party feels victimized. Therefore, if they felt wronged by Kennedy, why let him live for almost two and a half more years? That does not make any sense. Also, logistically speaking, it would be difficult for this group to pull off an overseas operation, since they operate exclusively within Israel. A final point to make to argue against their involvement is what amounts to near definitive proof of the participation of the military industrial complex in the cover up of the crime scene. In part two, we will see how the recovery of the emergency locator beacon proved that the U.S. government was involved in this conspiracy to assassinate John F. Kennedy, Jr.

Even if these reasons do not convince the skeptical reader that Shin Bet had nothing to do with the assassination, there is another line of thinking that we can pursue that could put them in the position of a support role. No doubt this article was not well received within the C.I.A. It showed Kennedy's willingness to support conspiracy theories, and his ability to look beyond manufactured patsies to see the truth, much like with his father's assassination. The article also may have alerted the C.I.A. to the existence of a potential partner.

The C.I.A. has a long, documented history of working with people and organizations who they share a common enemy with to engage in warfare and nefarious deeds. Examples include using the mafia to help run drugs, or attempt various times to assassinate Fidel Castro. Saddam Hussein and Osama bin Laden were funded by C.I.A. backing in the 1980s to fight the Iranians and the Russians. As we mentioned earlier, E. Howard Hunt said that at least one of the assassins, the shooter on the grassy knoll, was a French recruit named Lucien Sarti. The reason the agency does this is because if it ever was found out who was behind these assassinations, or operations, they can just blame the other entity. Very few people like the mafia anyway, for example, so they are a convenient scapegoat. And if in this case the assassination somehow got traced back to the Israelis, it could be written off as a terrorist attack. Using a middle man for an assassination is appealing because it blurs the lines of connection back to the C.I.A. Therefore, if Shin Bet wanted to assassinate Kennedy, they might have to enlist allied elements within Mossad, the Israeli foreign intelligence service to organize a plot. Mossad would then contact the C.I.A. to execute the plan. Another way this could have happened would be the other way, where the C.I.A. contacts either Mossad or Shin Bet and asks them for some explosives experts who might want to work on a contract, maybe not even naming who the target was. Or perhaps the C.I.A. specifically names Kennedy, knowing Israeli intelligence would be equally interested in silencing him.

The question then becomes, has there ever been any cooperation between Israeli intelligence and the C.I.A. to execute any missions, especially within the United States? Keep in mind, Israel has been a key American ally for decades, sharing intelligence for half a century. This from enclopedia.com: "Mossad agents managed in 1956 to obtain the full record of Nikita Khrushchev's famous speech at the Twentieth Congress of the Soviet Communist Party, in which some of the horrors of Stalin's rule were disclosed. This was shared with a grateful CIA in Washington... Over the years, the Mossad managed to capitalize on its widespread image as one of the world's most efficient intelligence agencies and created close relationships with many other national agencies, not the least important of which was that with the CIA." This relationship has never been broken over the decades. February 12, 2008, the *Washington Post* detailed a joint operation between the two spy agencies.

Imad Mughniyah, Hezbollah's international operations chief, walked on a quiet nighttime street in Damascus after dinner at a nearby restaurant. Not far away, a team of CIA spotters in the Syrian capital was tracking his movements. As Mughniyah approached a parked SUV, a bomb planted in a spare tire on the back of the vehicle exploded, sending a burst of shrapnel across a tight radius. He was killed instantly. The device was triggered remotely from Tel Aviv by agents with Mossad, the Israeli foreign intelligence service, who were in communication with the operatives on the ground in Damascus. "The way it was set up, the U.S. could object and call it off, but it could not execute," said a former U.S. intelligence official.

One final point we could make is that Mossad and the C.I.A. may have wanted to kill JFK, Jr., because they did the same thing to his father. There is speculation that Israeli intelligence conspired with the C.I.A. to assassinate President Kennedy in a support role. Perhaps this article was a sign that JFK, Jr., knew of this potential link and might one day expose it. The theory of an Israeli link to the JFK assassination was put forward by Press TV.

According to an American scholar and researcher, former US President Lyndon B. Johnson and former CIA chief Allen Dulles, along with Israel's Mossad and members of the military-industrial complex, are responsible for the assassination of President John F. Kennedy. Dr. Kevin

Barrett, a founding member of the Scientific Panel for the Investigation of 9/11, made the remarks in a phone interview with Press TV... Dr. Barrett said Israel had a motive to kill Kennedy because the president was opposed to the regime's nuclear weapons program which he believed could instigate a nuclear arms-race in the Middle East. Kennedy encountered tensions with former Israeli Prime Minister David Ben-Gurion who wanted to develop nuclear weapons, he said. "It seems very likely that indeed the Israelis played a significant role in the assassination as discussed in the Michael Collins Piper's book, *Final Judgment: The Missing Link in the JFK Assassination Conspiracy,*" the scholar observed.

We do not need to get too much further down this rabbit hole. The links here are tenuous. Shin Bet would not have the operational resources to do this overseas. The gripe with Kennedy was with them, not Mossad. I also have never heard of an assassination plot that takes nearly two and a half years to plan. These are the best spy agencies in the world. If they want someone dead, they can be put to death within a matter of hours. Still if some level of involvement by Israeli intelligence was present in Kennedy's death, it is not beyond the realm of possibility that they could have been enlisted because they shared a common enemy, and therefore may have had a hand in the death of John F. Kennedy, Jr. You could ask Michael Collins Piper if Israel had any role with the C.I.A. in killing President Kennedy, except you cannot any more. Piper died mysteriously in a hotel room at age 55 on June 1, 2015. No one should make any apologies for his repulsive white nationalism, yet when anyone dies so comparatively young under suspicious circumstances, it makes you question who wanted him dead. Let us not speak ill of the dead, yet the world is better off hearing no more of his anti-Semitic views. May he rest in peace and be the last of any mysterious deaths linked to the Kennedy assassinations.

# Part II

# The Watered-Down Version Sinks

Proving that John F. Kennedy, Jr.'s, death was an assassination and not just a tragic accident will require a single-minded approach to uncover the truth. Dismantling the official version of events put forward by the government, and the mainstream media, will be the purpose of the second part of this book. Having established a motive on the part of the C.I.A., and the Bush family, to eliminate Kennedy, let us examine the plot to eliminate JFK, Jr. Every possible angle must be examined so not a single skeptic can say that their point of view has any merit to it. I will strive for not a solitary flaw in my argumentation.

## Chapter Four

# The Myth of Spatial Disorientation

Let us start with the official explanation for what happened around 9:41 p.m. on July 16, 1999. After almost a year of investigation on July 6, 2000, the National Transportation and Safety Board issued a press release that summarized its findings.

> The National Transportation Safety Board today released its final report on the crash of a Piper Saratoga II aircraft last summer that killed the pilot, John F. Kennedy, Jr.; his wife, Carolyn Bessette Kennedy; and her sister, Lauren Bessette. The airplane crashed about 9:41 p.m., on July 16, 1999, near Martha's Vineyard, Massachusetts. The probable cause of the accident, as stated in the accident report, is: "The pilot's failure to maintain control of the airplane during a descent over water at night, which was a result of spatial disorientation. Factors in the accident were haze and the dark night." The accident report may be accessed through the aviation synopses page on the NTSB website. The NTSB accident number is NYC99MA178.

Therefore, several questions then need to be raised. Was Kennedy under the spell of spatial disorientation during the time of the crash? If he was not, that proves this crash was no accident. Was he an inexperienced pilot, given to taking unnecessary risks? Was he in any physical discomfort during the flight due to his recently fractured ankle? Is the stated time of the accident (9:41 p.m.) accurate? Was there any haze over Martha's Vineyard on the night of July 16, 1999? Is there any evidence of an explosion in the sky at the time of the accident? Was the fuel shutoff valve sabotaged? What does the wreckage site tell us about how the plane went down? Did the emergency rescue beacon go off at the time of impact, and if so, why did it take so long to recover the wreckage?

Let us first define spatial disorientation. For anyone who has ever driven their car off the road in a blizzard when there is zero visibility, then you might have fallen victim to this life-threatening mental state. I have done so myself. Fortunately, I landed in a forgiving snow bank, and no one was injured. A pilot suffering the same condition unfortunately cannot rely on such a soft landing. The encyclopedia *Britannica* defines this terrifying phenomenon as follows:

> Spatial disorientation, the inability of a person to determine his true body position, motion, and altitude relative to the earth or his surroundings. Both airplane pilots and underwater divers encounter the phenomenon. Most clues with respect to orientation are derived from sensations received from the eyes, ears, muscles, and skin. The human sensory apparatus, however, is often not delicate enough to perceive slow and gradual changes in motion; also, when motion changes are abrupt, the sense organs tend to overestimate the degree of change. Spatial disorientation in aircraft can arise from flight situations or visual misinterpretation. Banks and turns often create false sensations. When turning gradually, a pilot may feel as though he were on a straight course but ascending; when a turn is corrected, the impression is that of descending. If the plane banks or ascends or descends slowly, the pilot may not perceive the change, and the plane will feel level to him. If the plane skids while turning, the sensation is one of being banked in the direction opposite from the skid. A reaction called "leans" is caused by level flight after a rapid roll; the inertia of the roll causes the body to lean in a direction opposite to the direction of turning even after the motion of the roll has been stopped. If the pilot rapidly looks

downward while turning, the so-called Coriolis effect occurs, in which the plane feels as though it is descending.

The usual reaction of the pilot is to pull back on the stick to raise the plane. In a spin, the illusion of nonmotion is created if the spin is continued long enough; when the pilot corrects the spin, he has the feeling of spinning in the opposite direction, and his natural reaction is to counter his corrective measures and go back into the original spinning pattern. This phenomenon is known as the "graveyard spin." The "graveyard spiral" results when the sensation of turning is lost in a banked turn. Because the pilot's instruments show that he is losing altitude, he may pull back on the stick and add power, thus inducing a spiral motion. The oculogyral illusion is created by acceleration and turning: a turning target watched by a pilot while turning himself appears to move faster than it is actually going; it may appear to continue to turn even after the pilot has stopped his motion and the target has stopped.

Another illusion is caused by forward acceleration: when a pilot takes off from land, the increased speed gives the impression of nosing the plane too high; to compensate the pilot may lower the nose and dive back to the ground. During a rapid deceleration, the nose of the plane appears to drop; if the pilot corrects this feeling by trying to gain more altitude, the plane stalls and goes into a spin. The gravitational forces on a pilot cause the oculoagravic illusions: a target watched by a pilot appears to rise if weightlessness occurs and appears to fall when gravity is increased.

Visual misinterpretations do not usually depend on acceleration factors or on the sense of equilibrium but, rather simply, on visual illusions. The autokinetic phenomenon is the apparent wandering of an object or spot of light; when following another plane at night, the pilot may have trouble distinguishing between real and apparent movements of the lead plane. If two planes are flying parallel and level but at different speeds, they give the pilots the illusion of turning. Ground lights can be mistaken for the horizon or stars; fixed beacon lights can be mistaken for another plane flying in formation. The only measures that can prevent spatial disorientation are thorough training and instrumentation.

The last sentence is key. Did Kennedy have proper training and knowledge of his instruments to prevent this from happening to him, and react accordingly if faced with this situation? The answer to these questions is unequivocally yes.

Perhaps the foremost expert on the death of John F. Kennedy, Jr., is Scott Meyers. He has spent years archiving and researching nearly every aspect of this case. He was interviewed for the program "Encounters with the Unexplained: The Kennedy Curse, JFK, Jr.'s, Death – Accident or Assassination?" The program aired February 15, 2002, about two-and-a-half-years after the plane crash. He provided some essential testimony about the extensive training Kennedy had as a pilot, and the wide-ranging acumen he possessed with the instruments in the cockpit. It is useful to quote from Scott Meyers at length to dismantle the myth that Kennedy was a reckless pilot, or lacked experience to deal with an in-flight emergency.

"Every personal flight instructor he ever had says he was very cautious when he flew, not the kind of guy to take unnecessary chances. All of this goes against the official story of both the NTSB investigators and the mainstream media," said Myers. "He first began taking flight lessons in the early 1980s, and by the time of his death had over 700 hours of total flight time." This puts an end to the notion that Kennedy was an inexperienced pilot. In fact, the official NTSB report on the crash confirms this with a specific date for when Kennedy began his training as a pilot, October 4, 1982. "A copy of the pilot's logbook that covered from October 4, 1982, to November 11, 1998, was provided to the

Safety Board. The pilot's most recent logbook was not located." That is almost 17 years of flight.

Meyers also explained the training Kennedy did to become a seasoned pilot. "He had completed the written test for instrument flight rating and the training for the inflight instrument rating test...The fact that Kennedy knew how to use his plane's navigational instruments casts serious doubt on the official explanation for the crash, because even if he had gotten lost, his knowledge of the plane's instruments would have allowed him to flip a switch and allow the autopilot to guide him to a short distance from his runway destination. A little haze should have never stopped him from landing safely," said Meyers.

Journalist Michael Daly of the *New York Daily News* did a profile of JFK, Jr., for the Sunday, July 18, 1999, edition of the newspaper. It was aptly titled, "Flying Truly Was His Passion." In it, Daly discussed how being a pilot allowed him to escape the pressures of his high-profile life. "It gave him the peace he was looking for," said Kennedy's flight instructor Ralph Howard. "He got hounded wherever he went, and I think he realized this was where he could get away from everything. Nobody bothered him. It was so peaceful up there for him." Therefore, it is simply counterintuitive to suggest he was an inexperienced pilot when he seemed to want nothing more than to find an excuse to get back in the sky for stress relief. It is reminiscent of his father's love of sailing. "For 45 minutes, John Kennedy was able to be simply himself. He could admire the sunset and feel the wind as he would have no matter who his father had been. Many others had thrilled at the freedom of flight, but maybe no one ever needed it so much."

Howard also put to rest any notion that Kennedy was a reckless pilot. In fact, he was the opposite, especially when loved ones were on board. According to Daly, "on Nov. 25, 1997, three days after the 34th anniversary of his father's assassination, Kennedy traveled with his wife to Indiana to trade in the Buckeye for a two-seater. Howard and his brother Chris noted that Kennedy had become a careful pilot, always conducting a meticulous pre-flight check. 'Every nut and bolt on the airplane,' Chris Howard remembers. 'He was very safety oriented.'"

Daly also noted that Kennedy's love of flying became infectious with his wife. "Chris Howard took Carolyn Bessette Kennedy up for a flight in the two-seater. She threw her arms up and shouted like she was on a roller coaster. 'She said, 'I see now why John likes it so much,' Chris Howard remembers. After landing, she literally was jumping up and down with excitement. She and Kennedy ran toward each other. 'They just hugged and kissed,' Chris Howard says. 'Big smiles and laughing.'"

Daly also reported how easily Kennedy got his pilot's license. "After Kennedy headed back East, he stayed in touch with Ralph Howard by phone and E-mail. Kennedy reported that his wife was asking to go along whenever he went flying. 'She loved it, and he loved it,' Ralph Howard says. Kennedy himself sounded as excited as ever when he spoke of taking flight lessons in Vero Beach, Fla. He had no trouble getting the pilot's license needed for bigger planes in May 1998. 'John was a natural in flying,' Ralph Howard says."

On July 21, 1999, *USA Today* published an article titled "Pilot Kennedy was 'conscientious guy,'" co-written by Alan Levin, Kevin Johnson, and Deborah Sharp. The lead paragraph sought to dismiss the initial reporting of Kennedy as being inexperienced or reckless. "John F. Kennedy Jr. attended the Harvard of flight schools, may have had far more flight experience than has been reported and was known at his New Jersey airport for prudence in the cockpit," they reported. The article quoted many people who knew Kennedy as a good pilot.

"He was such a conscientious guy. I think it is way too early to speculate that he was at fault," says Harold Anderson, chief pilot at Mac Dan Aviation, a charter company based at the Essex County

Airport in Fairfield, N.J., where Kennedy began his flight Friday night. "A million things could have happened. People need to back off." Anderson and others at the Essex County Airport saw a different side of the young pilot. As recently as two months ago, Kennedy scrapped plans to fly himself and his wife to New England after he discovered an electrical problem on board his Cessna 182. Kennedy owned the Cessna prior to purchasing the Saratoga. His enthusiasm for flying bubbled over, they say, and he soon began sitting up in the co-pilot's seat, where he would watch the pilot and pick up pointers. "He dove into it," recalls Barry Stott, president of Air New England Inc. charter service. Stott had flown the Kennedys for years. Although he obtained his pilot's license in April 1998, Kennedy had been taking flying lessons for at least 10 years. Arthur Marx, who teaches flying at Martha's Vineyard Airport, says he gave Kennedy lessons 10 times over that period. "He was a good pilot," Marx says. "He wasn't the least bit cocky."

The NTSB report also noted that he had flown this route many times. "In the 15 months before the accident, the pilot had flown about 35 flight legs either to or from the Essex County/ Teterboro, New Jersey, area and the Martha's Vineyard/Hyannis, Massachusetts, area. The pilot flew over 17 of these legs without a CFI on board, including at least five at night. The pilot's last known flight in the accident airplane without a CFI on board was on May 28, 1999." The NTSB report also added this impressive anecdote of Kennedy's ability to recover from a simulated emergency. "On April 22, 1998, the pilot passed his private pilot flight test. The designated pilot examiner who administered the checkride stated that as part of the flight test, the pilot conducted two unusual attitude recoveries. The pilot examiner stated that in both cases, the pilot recovered the airplane while wearing a hood and referencing the airplane's flight instruments." A little haze over Martha's Vineyard, where Kennedy had flown over many times before at night and without a flight instructor, therefore would never have fazed him. He also never would have taken off if he thought the weather conditions were unfavorable. His experience and training would have allowed him to handle the situation, and use autopilot if needed.

It is also doubtful that there was any haze over Martha's Vineyard that night anyway. The Federal Aviation Administration hired an expert to determine what the weather conditions were on July 16, 1999, over Martha's Vineyard. Federal Aviation Administration Flight Specialist Edward Meyer of LaGuardia Airport in Queens N.Y., was appointed by FAA administrator Jane Garvey to study the weather conditions for July 16, 1999. His determination was that the conditions were at least very good. Meyer even issued a separate statement to make clear that he felt the conditions that night were anything but life threatening. He was forced to issue this additional statement when some media outlets contradicted his findings and reported that he had said the conditions were bad. Meyer stated, "Nothing of what I have heard on mainstream media makes any sense to me...The weather along his flight was just fine. A little haze over eastern Connecticut. I don't know why the airplane crashed, but what I heard on the media was nothing but garbage."

If the weather was fine, and Kennedy knew how to use his instruments, the conditions that create spatial disorientation did not exist. In fact, we can confirm that Kennedy was fine in the cockpit less than two minutes before the crash. The time of the crash is subject to much debate. The FAA official report says 9:41 p.m. as stated above in their press release. ABC News with Peter Jennings disputed this time, reporting that the plane disappeared at "9:40 p.m." Either way, the plane crash seems to have occurred no later than 9:41 p.m. This is important because Kennedy was in complete command of the aircraft as late as 9:39 p.m., experiencing no spatial disorientation. We know this because he contacted the Martha Vineyard's airport, asking permission to land as he was on approach at 9:39 p.m. If he or the aircraft were in distress he would have asked for help at this point. Kennedy did not.

"Within hours after the crash, a representative of the U.S. Coast Guard confirmed on air to a TV station in Boston that Kennedy had contacted the Martha's Vineyard Airport less than two minutes before the plane disappeared from radar," said Scott Meyers. "In this last contact, Kennedy was calm and collected as he requested permission to land at the small airport. He even told the air traffic controller he planned to drop off his sister-in-law and then take off for Hyannis Airport at around 11 p.m. And the TV station in Boston was not the only station to run the story. U.P.I. (United Press International), reported the same information."

Investigative reporter John A. Quinn researched this matter further and found that the tapes confirming this call to the Boston TV station had been scrubbed. "A NewsHawk associate has now obtained solid evidence that JFK, Jr., did in fact make radio contact with flight controllers at 9:39 p.m., July 16. What's even more important however, is that our associate also obtained irrefutable proof that the reported fact of this radio contact was deliberately removed from archived tape transcripts of WCVB-TV Channel 5's broadcast of July 17, 1999, during which – at approximately 12:35 PM – U.S. Coast Guard Petty Officer Todd Burgun reported to WCVB the fact of JFK, Jr.'s, radio contact the night before," said Quinn. "By later in the evening on July 17 this vital information was being actively covered up by WCVB and some other mass media outlets, as it has been in all subsequent government and mass media reports." Author Jim Marrs, perhaps the foremost expert on the JFK assassination has also researched the death of JFK, Jr., as well. He has reached the conclusion that the death of John F. Kennedy, Jr., was also an assassination. He was interviewed, like Scott Meyers, for the "Encounters with the Unexplained" program. Kennedy's contact with air traffic control is key to the entire narrative.

"The means he was not lost," said Marrs. "He was descending on approach to the airport. Seconds later, radar showed his plane dropped more than 1,000 feet in a manner of seconds. This means something catastrophic happened to that airplane."

In fact, it makes logical sense that Kennedy would have called in to air traffic control at 9:39 p.m. It would have been strange if he did not. According to ABC News with Peter Jennings, Kennedy's projected time of arrival was 10 p.m. at Martha's Vineyard Airport. Jennings reported that the radio tower closed at 10 p.m., so Kennedy was running out of time to ask for permission to land. Therefore, at 9:39 p.m., when Kennedy called in to air traffic control, he was just a few miles from his destination. A call at this point in the flight makes sense given where he was in the flight path.

Marrs also brought his expertise as a reporter into his analysis of this crash. During his time as a newspaper reporter in Texas, he covered many light commercial plane crashes. He noted that before any bodies were washed up, luggage was found on the shore. According to Marrs, this means that the cabin had been breached. In typical light commercial crashes when the cabin is not breached, the plane is crunched together with its bodies and luggage. Because luggage was found outside and far from the crash site, this indicates that something internally breached the cabin.

This fact can be easily verified. NBC News reported on the air on July 17, 1999, that luggage had been washed up at Gay Head, now called Aquinnah. Petty Officer Brent Herb of the U.S. Coast Guard confirmed on the air to NBC News that a piece of luggage was found floating about 200 yards off Gay Head. The point of last radar contact at sea at around 9:40 p.m. to Gay Head is nearly two miles. The obvious conclusion to make here is that there was an explosion on the plane that caused the crash and the internal breaching of the cabin. In the next chapter, we will deal with the extensive eyewitness evidence of an explosion, and the hunt to find the witnesses.

NBC News was not the only outlet to report debris being found, which would indicate a breaching of the cabin. ABC News with Peter Jennings reported the same information on the air during the afternoon of July 17, 1999, but was much more specific. It is hard to discount this information given the credibility of the source, and its specificity. Jennings said that the Police Chief of West Tisbury had called in to ABC News to report that they had recovered some luggage. Not only that, the chief said it was the luggage of Lauren Bessette, Kennedy's sister-in-law. This is an amazing piece of information. That means that the police chief took the time at the scene of the recovery to make sure it was luggage from the crash before calling in his report. It is also possible that the explosion had forced open the contents of the luggage so violently that he could easily verify who it beloved to. West Tisbury is two miles "up island" on Martha's Vineyard from Gay Head, so this is not the same luggage reported recovered by Brent Herb at Gay Head. Jennings also reported that the Coast Guard recovered a wheel and a sneaker, but would not immediately confirm it was from the downed aircraft.

## Chapter Five

# The Mistaken Rescue Beacon – The Best Evidence for a Conspiracy

More evidence of a conspiracy to assassinate John F. Kennedy, Jr., can be found in the aftermath of the crash, during the recovery effort. ABC News with Peter Jennings reported in the afternoon of July 17, 1999, on the air that a rescue beacon had been detected by the Coast Guard at 2:15 a.m. Initially this was reported as the rescue beacon for the Piper Saratoga, but then ABC News and other outlets had to retract that assumption and reported that in fact it was not from the Kennedy aircraft.

Conspiracy author, editor, and publisher Kenn Thomas has done extensive research on the issue of the rescue beacon. Like Jim Marrs and Scott Meyers, he was interviewed for the program, "Encounters with the Unexplained," as I mentioned earlier in the analysis of the potential Israeli intelligence connection to the death of JFK, Jr. The involvement of the U.S. government in the cover-up detailed below may be the strongest indicator that this assassination was not planned overseas, but instead executed with brutal efficiency by the U.S. military industrial complex. Thomas' analysis of the recovery effort leads him to believe that a cover-up of the evidence of a bomb took place at the crash scene. Taking that point further, if there was a cover-up, like with the JFK assassination, then there had to be a conspiracy within the United States.

Did the Piper Saratoga rescue beacon activate, like it should have, when the plane hit the water? It must have. Consider this bit of reporting by John Springer of the *Hartford Courant* on July 18, 1999. "It was equipped with an Emergency Locator Transmitter, or ELT, a device that is designed to send out a signal on a pre-designated frequency if the aircraft is involved in a sudden impact." And if this was so, why did it take so long to locate the wreckage if the plane went down at 9:41 p.m.? According to Thomas, the United States Navy initially said they heard the beacon loud and clear and were closing in on it. In fact, all throughout most of the initial coverage of the crash, most news outlets reported the discovery of the beacon. ABC News with Peter Jennings said it was first picked up at 2:15 a.m. on Saturday, July 17, 1999. Then according to Thomas, the Navy said it was not the signal from the Piper Saratoga. They had made a mistake. It was instead a distress signal from a downed Naval military aircraft. This was a stunning development, that has enormous implications.

Thomas did extensive studying, comparing sounds that would come from a Naval distress beacon as opposed to the sound that would come from the Piper Saratoga. In short, there would be no way to confuse them. The emergency rescue beacon of the Piper Saratoga has a shrill high pitch. This is vastly different than a military aircraft distress beacon which is deeper, and much louder, like a fog horn. The Navy would have been able to easily identify its own distress beacon, and not mistake it with a commercial aircraft. Taking this point further there are two logical conclusions here. One has to be the truth. The distress signal had to come from the Piper Saratoga, or a downed military aircraft that just happened to crash at approximately the same time and place as the Kennedy airplane. Therefore, either the Navy is telling the truth and it was one of their planes, or they were lying, and it was in fact the Piper Saratoga. We need to appreciate the magnitude of either of one of these possibilities. Let us start with the assumption that the Navy was not lying, that they were telling the truth, that they somehow were mistaken and confused two entirely different rescue signals. If that is the case I would like to raise some serious, but obvious questions that not even Kenn Thomas thought to ask, nor importantly did the mainstream media.

If we do accept that it was the distress beacon of a downed military aircraft, who died in that crash? Were there any survivors? How many people were on the plane? How could there be a distress beacon from the Navy in the exact spot where Kennedy's plane went down? That is an amazing coincidence. Did the plane collide with Kennedy's plane intentionally? If we take the Navy at their word, one of their own Naval aircraft was issuing a distress signal at the same time Kennedy's plane was missing. Then the story just went away. If they were telling the truth, what mission were they flying? If the pilot or pilots died, were the families notified? What caused them to crash? Was this an unmanned aircraft that was used to take down the Piper Saratoga with a bomb, or a direct hit to its fuselage? The C.I.A. was using highly accurate drones in a variety of ways in the 1990s, including the Predator Drone that could be mounted with a weapon, sent to collide with a target, or take photographs. Here is a summary of what the C.I.A. Predator could do courtesy of Ian G. R. Shaw from his book *Predator Empire: Drone Warfare and Full Spectrum Dominance:*

The Predator drone extended the GNAT's (a previous drone the C.I.A. used) limited range with the addition of a Ku-band SATCOM data ink. The new satellite communications overcame the limited data link of the GNAT and the limitations of the C-band line-of-sight. In fact, a SATCOM link meant that American drone operators didn't even have to be in same region or even continent as the drone. The Predator drones were first flown in June 1994, and were deployed to the Balkans under Operation Nomad Vigil and Operation Deliberate Force in 1995, the latter the name for the NATO air campaign against Bosnian Serb forces. Both the GNAT-750 and its offspring the Predator served simultaneously due the massive demand placed on surveillance aircraft. Future developments of the Predator included a de-icing system, reinforced wings, and a laser-guided targeting system: the latter two improvements were essential for weaponizing the drone in its later life.

We do know that the C.I.A. was conducting surveillance of the crash site by its own admission. Was there was a downed military aircraft issuing a distress signal at 2:15 a.m. in the waters off Martha's Vineyard? If there was, the Navy covered up that crash, who was involved with it, and what role it may have played in the evening's events. A large obstacle to believing that there was a downed military aircraft is what to do with the bodies, and notifying the family, or families, of the downed airmen. This would require a conspiracy of vast proportions to pull that off.

The alternative is equally troubling. Thomas concludes that instead, the simpler explanation here is what happened. In other words, the Navy lied. There was no downed military aircraft floating in the waters off Martha's Vineyard at 2:15 a.m. on July 17, 1999. It was the Piper Saratoga issuing its rescue beacon as logic would obviously dictate. Why would the Navy lie about this though? The answer is to buy themselves more time. Thomas notes that the military immediately instituted in the hours after the crash a 17-nautical mile no file zone, and no entry zone, around the crash site. No civilians or media were allowed in this area until the bodies and wreckage were recovered. Thomas believes this allowed the military time to destroy any evidence of a bomb on the aircraft, or any other inconvenient proof of anything other than the official story of events. If the 2:15 a.m. rescue beacon really was from the Piper Saratoga there would be no reason to lie about it unless you were trying to cover something up. That we are led to believe the Navy could not detect the sound of its own rescue beacon would be a stunning example of incompetence on the part of the entire crew.

In a final ignominy to this tragic part of the tale it is not lost on me that John F. Kennedy nearly gave his life for his country fighting in World War II for the U.S. Navy. This irony was probably not lost on the part of the plotters. Perhaps that is why the C.I.A. chose the Navy to help carry out this plot on domestic soil, where it is illegal for them to operate.

In looking at the evidence here it seems obvious that the Navy covered something up here, either the crash of a military aircraft, or the early recovery of the Piper Saratoga. Because they took part in one of these cover ups, this is the clearest sign of the involvement of the military industrial complex in this assassination. Had Kennedy's Piper Saratoga not been equipped with a state of art emergency locator beacon we may never have been able to get to the truth.

## Chapter Six

# The Mystery of the Fuel Selector Valve

One of the most interesting pieces of evidence that could point to the fact that the Piper Saratoga was sabotaged was tucked away deep within the NTSB report.

The fuel selector valve was recovered, and the bottom of the valve was missing. All three fuel line connections were broken off. The valve had separated from the fuselage attach points. The selector valve linkage was deformed, and the valve was found in the OFF position.

The Federal Aviation Administration, in their official policies and regulations handbook, describes the role of the fuel selector valve in the following way:

> There must be a means to allow appropriate flight crew members to rapidly shut off the fuel to each engine individually in flight. No shutoff valve may be on the engine side of any firewall. There must be means to guard against inadvertent operation of each shutoff valve and means to reopen each valve rapidly after it has been closed. Each valve and fuel system control must be supported so that loads resulting from its operation, or from accelerated flight conditions, are not transmitted to the lines connected to the valve. Gravity and vibration should not affect the selected position of any valve. Fuel valve handles and their connections to valve mechanisms must have design features that minimize the possibility of incorrect installation. Check valves must be constructed to preclude incorrect assembly or connection of the valve. Fuel tank selector valves must require a separate

and distinct action to place the selector in the OFF position. The tank selector positions must be located in such a manner that it is impossible for the selector to pass through the OFF position when changing from one tank to another.

The key line here is "fuel tank selector valves must require a separate and distinct action to place the selector in the OFF position." There would be no reason, not to mention being close to impossible for Kennedy to sabotage his fuel lines during the middle of the flight. If he did not turn the fuel selector switch to off, then who did? The two other women on the plane would not even be able to locate the valve, having no instrument, or pilot training. Therefore, if none of the three people on the plane would logically ever touch the valve, we are left with the only possible conclusion. Someone outside the plane turned the switch to off after the crash. But why? Perhaps to make it look like Kennedy was an inexperienced pilot, even idiotic, or that he was committing suicide. It is unlikely that he was committing suicide since he called into air traffic control to tell the airport that he was dropping off his sister-in-law. And why would he pack luggage for the weekend wedding they were going to attend, or tell the air traffic control that after he dropped off Lauren, he and Caroline were heading north to the party. That sure does not sound like someone who is going to kill himself. The most likely scenario is that the switch was set to off when the Navy and the Coast Guard recovered the wreckage in secret without the watchful eyes of the media with the intent to disparage the reputation of Kennedy as a pilot. We also could hazard the possibility that an explosion or the impact of the crash could have caused this. This seems unlikely though because changing the valve requires two separate and distinct actions. In the end, this part of the story is probably one we will never be able to clearly answer. All we do know is that the valve was allegedly found to be off, but maybe even that was a lie. With the mystery of the fuel selector valve there seems to be more questions than answers.

## Chapter Seven

# The Mysterious Flight Instructor

In some of the early reporting of the crash, there was speculation that Kennedy had either refused a flight instructor to accompany him on the flight, or that one had perished in the crash. We can rule out the idea that a flight instructor died in the crash. It would be impossible for any of Kennedy's well known and gifted flight instructors to have perished in this plane crash, and not be widely reported within that community, much less within the family of such of a person. That would be two groups of people, one personal, and the other professional, that could number in the hundreds who would have to be silenced somehow. The very idea is ludicrous.

This leaves us with the notion that he refused a certified flight instructor to board the plane. Even if he did it would have made no difference. He successfully flew the plane for an hour with no help on this routine flight as we established before. He had already done this five times in the dark without a flight instructor. The whole notion of a mysterious flight instructor dying on board, or him refusing a flight instructor were both intended to make him look reckless. If there was a certified flight instructor on board, the media could say that he was such a bad pilot, even the help of a flight instructor could not save him. Or if he refused one, it would show that he lacked good judgement, and was unable to fly the plane on his own. We already dispelled the notion many times over that Kennedy was an inexperienced, or reckless pilot. The story of Kennedy refusing help was a key part of the narrative to discredit him, so I would like to examine this further to find out what really happened here.

This is from ABC News on July 7, 2000: "John F. Kennedy Jr. turned down an offer by one of his flying instructors to accompany him the night of his fatal flight to Martha's Vineyard, saying he 'wanted to do it alone,' federal investigators say." This is from the *Los Angeles Times* on the same day: "John F. Kennedy Jr. turned down an offer by one of his flying instructors to accompany him the night of his doomed flight to Martha's Vineyard, saying that he 'wanted to do it alone,' federal investigators reported Thursday." The *New York Times* reported it this way: "One of his flight instructors offered to fly with him that night, but Mr. Kennedy said 'he wanted to do it alone,' the instructor told the investigators who prepared the report."

Here is the relevant section in the NTSB report.

The CFI stated that the pilot had the ability to fly the airplane without a visible horizon but may have had difficulty performing additional tasks under such conditions. He also stated that the pilot was not ready for an instrument evaluation as of July 1, 1999, and needed additional training. The CFI was not aware of the pilot conducting any flight in the accident airplane without an instructor on board. He also stated that he would not have felt comfortable with the accident pilot conducting night flight operations on a route similar to the one flown on, and in weather conditions similar to those that existed on, the night of the accident. The CFI further stated that he had talked to the pilot on the day of the accident and offered to fly with him on the accident flight. He stated that the accident pilot replied that "he wanted to do it alone."

There are several suspicious aspects to this. One obvious point is that this certified flight instructor was never given a name in this report, nor by ABC News, the *New York Times*, the *Los Angeles Times*, or any other news outlet that reported it. I find that highly suspicious. Of all the flight instructors who knew Kennedy, it would logically be this person that the media would want to track down. He could further the myth that Kennedy was a reckless pilot. He would be perfect for the official version of events. He could have given key information about JFK's health, state of mind, and other last words Kennedy may have had. Also, this man, if this story is true, should be dead. He of course would have perished in the crash as well. You would think there would be a race to find out who this person was, and his thoughts on cheating death. The finest news gathering organizations never bothered to track him down, or verify this unnamed source in the NTSB report, just taking the government at their word.

Another strikingly unusual aspect to the anonymous CFI is that he (or she) is the only instructor in the report, or in subsequent media reports, who had negative things to say about Kennedy as a pilot. As we saw earlier, all of Kennedy's flight instructors glowed about him including Harold Arnold, and Arthur Max. One example was discussed in the NTSB report from a different CFI. "The CFI (certified flight instructor) had made six or seven flights to MVY (Martha's Vineyard Airport) with the pilot in the accident airplane. The CFI stated that most of the flights were conducted at night and that, during the flights, the pilot did not have any trouble flying the airplane. The instructor stated that the pilot was methodical about his flight planning and that he was very cautious about his aviation decision-making. The CFI stated that the pilot had the capability to conduct a night flight to MVY as long as a visible horizon existed."

Therefore, it seems unusual that this mystery person was saying such strikingly bad things about Kennedy that go against the ponderous amount of evidence to the contrary. He also seems amazingly ignorant of Kennedy's flight history. "The CFI was not aware of the pilot conducting any flight in the accident airplane without an instructor on board." Remember this from the NTSB report? "In the 15 months before the accident, the pilot had flown about 35 flight legs either to or from the Essex County/Teterboro, New Jersey, area and the Martha's Vineyard/

Hyannis, Massachusetts, area. The pilot flew over 17 of these legs without a CFI on board, including at least 5 at night." He also seems curiously critical about Kennedy's ability to use the plane's instruments, saying he needed additional training. Perhaps he wasn't aware of Kennedy's demonstrated ability to successfully use his instruments blind, with a hood on.

If this anonymous person even did exist, he seems to have had only a tenuous relationship with Kennedy at best, having little knowledge of his flight history, or repeated successful flights using instruments without a flight instructor. I find it unusual that not a single news organization thought to track this person down, and verify his supposed relationship with Kennedy. The story seems concocted to embarrass Kennedy and make him look reckless. I mentioned before that this person is the only one of his flight instructors who had bad things to say about him. If he did exist it is possible they did not get along, and Kennedy did not respond well to his negative reinforcement. It is possible Kennedy did not feel comfortable with this individual on a personal level. His constant nagging and criticism may have made him feel uncomfortable while trying to pilot the plane. That may be why he said he wanted to do this "alone," a polite way of saying, "get lost." These are questions that could have been asked if any news organization thought to track down this infamous flight instructor who cheated death. That would be quite a story to tell. The fact that they never bothered to look for him might be our greatest clue of all that he never existed in the first place. The point also needs to be made that even if he did exist, Kennedy did not need a flight instructor that night, as demonstrated by his one hour of flight that he executed with expert precision.

# Chapter Eight

# Exactly one hour of flight

*Time* magazine reported in their cover story for July 26, 1999, the following information. "At 8:38 p.m...the Essex tower cleared them for take-off, and the wheels of the red-and-white Piper Saratoga left the ground." The NTSB report is even more specific. "At 2038:32, the pilot of N9253N contacted the tower controller and advised that he was ready to take off from runway 22. At 2038:39, the tower controller cleared N9253N for take-off; at 2038:43, the pilot acknowledged the clearance. A few seconds later, the tower controller asked the pilot if he was heading towards Teterboro, New Jersey. The pilot replied, 'No sir, I'm uh actually I'm heading a little uh north of it, uh eastbound.' The tower controller then instructed the pilot to 'make it a right downwind departure then.' At 2038:56, the pilot acknowledged the instruction stating, 'right downwind departure two two.'" It takes about four seconds to say, "right downward departure two two." Add those four seconds to 2038:56 (which in civilian terms means 56 seconds after 8:38 p.m.) and you arrive at 8:39 p.m. That means John F. Kennedy, Jr. finished his first conversation with air traffic control at exactly 8:39 p.m. as he was clearing the tower. This time of take-off has me even more convinced that Kennedy called into air traffic control at 9:39 p.m. Once 9:39 p.m. arrived, one hour into the flight, he would have begun the process of calling into air traffic control, with them receiving, or finishing the short call by 9:39 p.m. It makes sense, as a good pilot, he would report in to air traffic control once he had completed an hour of flight, and was also nearing his runway destination. This proves he was not picking a random time to call in, but choosing the one-hour marker to check in, as commercial airline pilots sometimes do. The time of the call-in corresponding to the exact time of take-off one hour before, leads me to be convinced of his 9:39 p.m. check-in even further. It was not a random time that he picked. It also shows his intense mental focus to be able to call in at the exact one-hour marker. If he was distracted or suffering spatial disorientation he would not have made this call, much less at precisely one hour into the flight. That is too much of a coincidence. He may have even begun calling in at 9:38 to finish by 9:39 p.m. to be even more precise. Either way, when we add this to the reports the Coast Guard, from Boston television, and United Press International, it gives us further proof that the crucial 9:39 p.m. call did exist. It proves that 9:39 p.m. was not a random time to call in.

The Essex County Airport is a short train ride or car ride to the New York City metro area. Kennedy was scheduled to drop off his sister-in-law Lauren Bessette at around 10 p.m. at the Martha's Vineyard Airport. Next, he would depart around 11 p.m. to head up to Hyannisport, to the Kennedy compound where his cousin Rory would be getting married the next day. We established earlier that the time of the crash was probably 9:40 p.m. or 9:41 p.m. at the latest, with Kennedy calling into air traffic control at 9:39 p.m. We can draw many important conclusions from this.

First, the entire flight time before the crash was approximately one hour, spanning from 8:38 p.m. to 9:41 p.m. It is impossible for someone who was experiencing spatial disorientation to successfully pilot the craft for an hour. Second, if there were any mechanical defects that caused this crash they would have shown up during these 60 minutes from take-off to his call into the Martha's Vineyard air traffic control tower. Also, if there were any mechanical problems with the plane, Kennedy would have reported them when he called into the tower. He did not ask for any help when he radioed in. Nothing was wrong with him, or the plane, at 9:39 p.m. Then, as Jim Marrs pointed out, the plane dropped over a thousand feet in a matter of seconds.

Therefore, this long flight time, plus Kennedy's call to air traffic requesting permission to land, prove that the condition of the pilot and the plane were functioning perfectly, as late 9:39 p.m., 60 or so minutes into the flight. Then catastrophe struck.

But why then? I think we can further prove that there was a bomb on that plane by when the bomb went off. It would be important to make sure that the device did not detonate over land. There would be the chance for far too many witnesses on the ground, and the potential for recovery of debris by civilians. The bomb had to detonate over open water so the area could be sealed off to civilians, and the wreckage could be recovered secretly as we noted earlier. A detonation over open water also minimizes the number of potential witnesses to the explosion, and witnesses to the weather conditions. If the bomb detonated over open land, anyone would know the weather conditions if they were standing there, but over open water they can be debated because of the lack of witnesses.

Therefore, one possible scenario includes a bomb placed on the airplane while it was hangered at the Caldwell Airstrip. A second possibility would be a heat-seeking sea to air missile launched from a boat's guided weaponry, or from a shoulder harness. A third possibility would be a mid-air collision with another aircraft, or a drone that sent the Kennedy plane into a nosedive. If a bomb was placed on the Piper Saratoga I see no problem with the C.I.A. doing so while the plane was housed at the Caldwell Airstrip in Fairfield, New Jersey. Christopher Anderson wrote in *The Day John Died*, that Kennedy had originally had his private plane at the busy Teterboro Airport in New Jersey where fellow celebrities like Harrison Ford and Bill Cosby had hangered their planes. He moved his Piper Saratoga to the Caldwell Airport in Fairfield, New Jersey, because the atmosphere there was much more informal and relaxed. Such a loose atmosphere would make it easy for anyone to come and go, posing as a maintenance person to place a bomb on the aircraft.

We also should mention the strange goings-on at the Caldwell Airport (also known as the Essex County Airport) in Fairfield, New Jersey, just two years after the Kennedy plane crash. The September 27, 2001, edition of *The New York Daily News* explained it best in an article titled "F.B.I. Suspects Terrorists Trained on Small Planes."

> Federal agents are investigating whether hijackers who steered two jets into the World Trade Center practiced their deadly routes in small rented planes. The F.B.I. has asked the operators of flight schools at the Essex County Airport in New Jersey if they rented planes to the hijackers in the weeks before the Sept. 11 attack. Special Agent Sandra Carroll, an F.B.I. spokeswoman in New Jersey, declined to discuss the test-flight scenario, other than to say the queries were part of a sweeping effort to retrace the hijackers' actions and contacts. "What we're trying to determine is what movements they may have had, what contacts," she said. If in fact they did do practice runs, how relevant is that right now from a criminal investigation standpoint? I don't know.

Carroll would not say which of the hijackers may have rented planes in New Jersey or how many flights they may have taken. Federal regulations require pilots of small planes operating under visual flight rules to stay below 1,100 feet along the East and Hudson rivers. The planes are not allowed to fly over Manhattan. Citing an unnamed investigator, *The Star-Ledger* of Newark reported that the owner of Caldwell Flight Academy told investigators he had recently rented planes to some of the hijackers – and that it was now believed they made practice runs or rehearsals near the Trade Center. People working at the school yesterday declined to comment. "The F.B.I. has been here," said a man who answered the phone at the Caldwell school. "They've been to every flight school in New Jersey."

"The 25-mile route from the Essex airport to lower Manhattan and along the island is popular with pilots. "Northbound you fly within 100 yards of the Trade Center," said Joe Orlando, who has flown out of Caldwell for the past five years. "You used to get a beautiful view of the towers, a view that in retrospect was probably too close."

We also know that the C.I.A. did not share information to anyone about what they knew about the 9/11 hijackers before the September 11, 2001 terrorist attacks. For example, ABC News in an article titled "CIA Didn't Share Info About 9/11 Hijackers," reported "given the CIA's failure to disseminate, in a timely manner, intelligence information on the significance and location of Al-Midhar and Alhamzi (two of the hijackers), that chance, unfortunately, never materialized." On September 14, 2001, *Newsweek* revealed that "U.S. military sources have given the F.B.I. information that suggests five of the alleged hijackers of the planes that were used in Tuesday's terror attacks received training at secure U.S. military installations in the 1990s."

To be clear, I do not know exactly what to make of the fact that some of the terrorists linked to the 9/11 attacks trained and took off from the same airport as Kennedy's fated flight. We do know that the C.I.A. was monitoring the terrorists long before the attacks, and the terrorists were trained at government facilities. I only brought up this line of inquiry to leave no stone unturned. In the final analysis, what we might learn from this is that if these terrorists could train that long at Fairfield, it does speak to the truly lax atmosphere at the airstrip where it seemed not to matter who was coming and going, even men who would attack our country, or even plant a bomb on an airplane.

## Chapter Nine

# Dealing with a fractured ankle

One excuse that has been put forward to suggest why Kennedy crashed his plane was that his ankle was too weak to be able to fly the aircraft. Kennedy did some paragliding with his Buckeye "powerparachute" and crashed it into a tree, fracturing his ankle in the spring of 1999. According to Kenn Thomas, this happened on Memorial Day weekend in 1999. He spent the next several weeks in recuperation, hobbling around New York City on crutches. His cast was removed a day before the plane crash, having completely healed. Memorial Day was May 31 in 1999. The NTSB report said the accident took place June 1, 1999. That gave him over 6 weeks to mend the fractured ankle, about 44 days. The cast obviously would not have been removed if his doctor did not feel the ankle was healed. One myth that we can dispel is that he was flying the airplane with a cast. That was not true.

All indications were that the ankle had healed. Kennedy got the cast removed Thursday morning, July 15, so he had all of Thursday and most of Friday to determine if he was well enough to fly. He spent Thursday night at the New York Yankees game, and apparently was well enough to get in a workout on Friday afternoon at his health club before the take-off of his flight. He also had a revealing conversation at a gas station just before he made his way to Caldwell Airstrip. *Time* magazine reported this telling encounter in its July 26, 1999, cover story.

Around 8:10 p.m., Kennedy pulled into the West Essex Sunoco station just across the street from the airport. Jack Tabibian, who owns the station, was accustomed to seeing Kennedy stop in when he came out to fly, but never this late.

"He usually showed up between 5 p.m. and 7 p.m.," Tabibian says. If J.F.K. Jr. was concerned about the late hour and the fast-setting sun, he didn't show it. Walking unhurriedly into the store wearing a light gray T-shirt, he made a bit of small talk with Mesfin Gebreegziabher, who was manning the cash register. Gebreegziabher asked after Kennedy's leg, and Kennedy reported it was feeling better.

*Time* then added this important observation about the take-off. "The take-off, to all appearances, was a smooth one, suggesting that Kennedy's still shaky ankle did not hamper his ability to operate the Piper's pedals." In fact, the greatest indicator that his ankle was just fine was the fact that he flew the airplane successfully for an entire hour with no problems. His call in to air traffic control at 9:39 p.m. reported no problems with the aircraft, or himself. Autopilot could handle any difficulties he might be having with the pitch of the wings, which is handled by the pedals. The only other time he would have to use the pedals would be for braking the Piper Saratoga on landing, which of course never happened. John Springer of the *Hartford Courant* reported the following interesting information about this particular Piper Saratoga, a 1995 model.

"For private pilots, it is a fairly sophisticated, high-performance aircraft," said John D. Kelly, president of East Haven-based Shoreline Aviation Inc. "It is a kind of high- end private airplane."' Kelly, an FAA license examiner who has been at the controls of Saratogas, said the aircraft responds well to pilot commands to turn, ascend and accelerate. "I think Piper airplanes in general are among the most docile airplanes,"' he said. "They have excellent handling characteristics.""

I feel confident in ruling out Kennedy's ankle as playing any role in this crash. He had plenty of time to heal, over six weeks, in fact. His doctor never would have removed the cast if the ankle was not ready. Kennedy spent the better part of two days testing the ankle, giving himself plenty of time to determine if it was strong enough. The fact that he did not go back to the doctor's office on Friday morning to have the cast put back on suggests the ankle was responding well to his busy routine, including getting in a workout on Friday afternoon. We also know that he told a convenience store worker that the ankle was "feeling better," just before take-off. Add to this the fact that the take-off went off without a hitch, as did an hour of flight with no problems reported on radar, or during his call in at 9:39 p.m. The obvious conclusion is that the ankle was fine and played no role in this crash.

We also ruled out spatial disorientation as being a cause of the crash. Kennedy's call in to air traffic control at 9:39 p.m. when he requests permission to land shows that he was in command of the aircraft, and himself. According his instructors he was a trained, careful, experienced pilot. He was flying a plane that was easy to use, including autopilot that he was trained to use if there was any sign of trouble. He was also flying in weather that posed no problems to himself, or the aircraft according to FAA investigator Edward Meyer. We also determined that the Navy covered up either the downing of one their own aircrafts, or that they lied about the time of finding the rescue beacon for the Piper Saratoga, either of which proves a cover-up.

If all of this is not enough to logically conclude that John F. Kennedy, Jr., was the victim of a conspiracy to assassinate him on the night of July 16, 1999, there is still more proof that can be examined to add to the evidence pile. If Kennedy did not drive his plane into the ocean because of his own pilot error, which we have concluded was not the case, then is there evidence that an explosion happened on the aircraft, to account for the Piper Saratoga plunging thousands of feet per second just after

Kennedy radioed in to air traffic control? The tantalizing answer to that question is yes. The truth lies in the eyewitness testimony of three people who happened to be in the right place at the right time to see the tragic truth of what brought down the Piper Saratoga. I did mention that the obvious signs of a cover-up in the recovery of the rescue beacon may be the best evidence for a conspiracy in this case. However, the collective weight of what these three people saw in the sky that night is at least equally compelling in building a case for an assassination. Let us find out who these people were, and the remarkable similarity in their stories.

## Chapter Ten

# Only the Vineyard Knows

The JFK assassination and the RFK assassination both can be proven to be conspiracies using eyewitness testimony. In both cases, credible people saw more than one person shooting at the crime scene. Although there was no gun involved in the JFK, Jr., plane crash (that we know of) we can still rely on eyewitness testimony to bring us closer to the truth. Three people heard an explosion in the sky near Martha's Vineyard on the night of July 16, 1999. This would contradict the official version of events that the plane crashed due to pilot error. Let us examine them one at a time.

Keep in mind, this section builds off the previous point made by Jim Marrs. The fact that luggage, (and possibly other debris) was found scattered miles away from the crash site, indicated that the cabin had been breached by an internal explosion. If eyewitness testimony could back up this claim, there would be no reasonable way to avoid concluding that a bomb brought down the Piper Saratoga.

## Eyewitness number one: The party guest

We will start with the one person with which there is the least information available about. Journalist Lawrence Patterson in the July 31, 1999, edition of the journal *Criminal Politics* reported the following information. "A report at 3:00 p.m. Saturday, by Shepard Smith of Fox TV, named another of these witnesses. In fact, the witness was a guest at the scheduled wedding that J.F.K., Jr., and his wife were on their way to attend. The witness was also a friend of Shepard Smith, who is a producer at Fox TV." In other references, this person is referred to as a friend or cousin of a producer at Fox News. Scott Meyers in his interview with "Encounters with the Unexplained," listed this person as well as being one of the three witnesses to an explosion in the sky.

"Several witnesses on the ground that night reported seeing and hearing an airborne explosion in the area where Kennedy's plane went down, and these were all very credible witnesses," said Meyers. This particular witness "was actually in town for Rory Kennedy's wedding which was to take place that weekend, the very event John and Caroline were headed for when their plane went down. These eyewitness stories were widely reported by all kinds of media outlets including United Press International, ABC News, and Fox TV."

Seeking to find out if I could uncover any further information about this person, I attempted to contact Shepard Smith at Fox News. I thought he might be willing to at least reflect on the coverage his network did for this tragic event, if nothing else for historical purposes. Such a request seemed innocuous enough. Then the plan was to broach the subject of this eyewitness account later. I sent one email to his show account as listed on the website, and the other to his personal account. Here is what I sent.

John Koerner <jpkoerner@yahoo.com>
To foxreport@foxnews.com
Mar 7, 2017, at 5:31 PM
Dear Mr. Smith:
I am writing to inquire if you would be willing to reflect back on the coverage Fox News did for the death of JFK Jr in July 1999 by answering a few questions I have. I am a professor of American history in Williamsville, N.Y. Thank you for your time.
Professor John Koerner

John Koerner <jpkoerner@yahoo.com>

To smith@foxnews.com

Mar 7, 2017, at 5:34 PM

Dear Mr. Smith:

I am writing to inquire if you would be willing to reflect back on the coverage Fox News did for the death of JFK Jr in July 1999 by answering a few questions I have. I am a professor of American history in Williamsville, N.Y. Thank you for your time.

Professor John Koerner

I have yet to receive any reply to either inquiry. I doubt I ever will.

## Eyewitness number two: The Mysterious Reporter from the *Martha's Vineyard Gazette*

The story of trying to track down the second witness to this airborne explosion is equally compelling as to what this witness had to say about the events of July 16, 1999. More on that hunt for his identity later. The second witness in question was a reporter for the *Martha's Vineyard Gazette* who was walking along the beaches of Martha's Vineyard that night, and just happened to be looking in the right place at the right time. What is important about this witness is that he both saw and heard an explosion.

Investigator Don Jeffries had this to say about this "mysterious reporter."

WCVB-TV reporter Steve Sbraccia, who covered the story, wrote in a 2006 email, "I've always felt there was something wrong about that crash...from the way the police swept through that beach forcing everyone off – to the way they kept the wreck site closely guarded until they pulled up every bit of debris...." Sbraccia had encountered the enigmatic reporter from the *Martha's Vineyard Gazette*, who claimed to have seen an explosion in the air and then seemingly vanished from the face of the earth. In another email to me, from 2012, Sbraccia reiterated, "I can swear in court that man was real – and I reported exactly what he told me he saw." Researcher John DiNardo had attempted to track down this elusive reporter shortly after the incident, but the paper refused to even furnish his name. I encountered the same resistance, when the present editor, who claimed to have personally covered the story for the paper, informed me that she had no recollection at all of the reports about a mid-air explosion, or of any such reporter.

Here is DiNardo's acount of his conversation with the *Vineyard Gazette*.

I just phoned the *Martha's Vineyard Gazette*, and spoke with a woman there. I asked her about the statement, in the early reports of the John F. Kennedy Jr. plane crash, that a reporter for the *Martha's Vineyard Gazette* had witnessed an explosion in the sky around the time of the crash. She replied, "Oh, that story was completely bogus. What really happened was that someone was shooting off fireworks on Falmouth." "Falmouth?" I said, "Is that an island?" "Falmouth," she said, "is the closest point to Martha's Vineyard." I said, "But this reporter witnessed an explosion in the SKY." She countered, "Well, they were shooting rockets up in the air, or something like that." Fearing that I might scare her off if I continued along this line of inquiry, I asked, "May I speak with the reporter who witnessed this?" "Oh, no," she replied nervously, "we can't do that." I said, "Oh, that's strange. What would be the problem with speaking to a reporter?" She repeated, "We can't permit that." I said, "Okay, can you at least give me his name?" "No, we can't do that, either," she persisted. Then she added, "He no longer works for us," almost as if she were making it up, just to turn me away. And then when I responded in a surprised "Ohhh," she suddenly realized that that comment made matters worse, and, in a jolt of vexation, she sputtered, "Oh, no, no – it has nothing to do with that incident; he went back to school." "Oh," I said, "so is he a journalism student?" After an answerless pause, I thanked her and said goodbye. I think she was relieved.

Notice that the truth finally comes out at the end of the interview when the editor felt suspicion may have been cast upon her, or the newspaper. At that point, she panicked and had to reveal that the reporter went back to school, and was not mysteriously missing, or fired for reporting the truth about the "incident" as she calls it. She also knows exactly who DiNardo was talking about. She also knows that this eyewitness went back to school, but will not say where. Her cover story about this explosion being fireworks from Falmouth is idiotic for several reasons. Each one of these three witnesses reported hearing a single explosion in the sky. The sound did not come from the water, so it was not the sound of the plane crashing. Also, Falmouth is in the opposite direction to where these witnesses where looking. Each one of them was looking west as they were strolling on the western end of Martha's Vineyard Island. It would be impossible to see or hear fireworks going off at Falmouth if you were standing on the western end of the Martha's Vineyard Island. You would have to turn completely around, look across the entire length of the island, and all of Vineyard Sound to see or hear anything going on in Falmouth. It is over 30 miles northeast from where the witnesses were located, a nearly two-hour commute by car and ferry. The crash site for Kennedy's plane was several miles out to the west if you were standing on the shore at Martha's Vineyard. When is the last time someone mistook the colors of fireworks for a single airborne explosion? Each one reported hearing a single explosion. This of course is something quite the opposite of multiple rockets being launched in Falmouth. That would be an entirely different event. Not one of these people reported multiple explosions. The Kennedy explosion site was in the opposite direction of Falmouth. Therefore, the editor is lying and sheltering this reporter for some unknown reason especially unusual if all he witnessed were some fireworks. If the story was "bogus" why be so guarded about the "incident" and refuse to give his name?

My suspicions were confirmed through my own research that the *Vineyard Gazette* has no interest in sharing more about this story, and maybe not just them. I wanted to see if I could find for myself who this reporter might be. The information to go on helps narrow down who to look for. You can first obviously eliminate all female reporters at the *Gazette* as being the person in question. Then you would look for someone whose name no longer appears in the newspaper after August 1999, or perhaps as late as early September 1999, when presumably this person would have gone back to school. If more than one male reporter disappears from the bylines after these months, it would be that much more difficult to determine exactly who this witness was. However, if only one male reporter was no longer producing bylines after these months, then logic would dictate that this person is the one in question. Keep in mind if this person was a student reporter they probably began working during May or June when school lets out, to begin an internship. Therefore, if you could find a male reporter who began writing for the *Gazette* in say, May or June 1999, and then stopped reporting for them in August or September 1999, it would confirm the information from John DiNardo's interview, and give us solid proof that this person did exist.

To do this requires looking at microfilm from the time in question. To be thorough, the period from April 1999 through October 1999 should be examined to see when and if any new staff members appeared and/or disappeared. Acquiring that microfilm from the *Vineyard Gazette* though was much more difficult than I expected. I would like to thank the staff at the Buffalo and Erie County Public Library (B&ECPL), and the Library of Congress, for their several months of relentless pursuit of this microfilm. The staff at the Grosvenor Room and the interlibrary loan department at the B&ECPL were indispensable in helping me track down this elusive film. The following is a record of the BECPL's repeated attempts to acquire this film.

3/22/2017 12:34:02 PM
Submitted by Customer
1000118797264
3/22/2017 12:34:02 PM
Awaiting Request Processing
1000118797264
3/23/2017 3:47:22 PM
Request in Processing
Tracy
3/23/2017 3:47:27 PM
Awaiting Request Processing
Tracy
3/24/2017 11:11:22 AM
Request in Processing
Isabell
3/24/2017 11:14:28 AM
Request Sent
Isabell
3/30/2017 10:22:36 AM
Awaiting Unfilled Processing
System
4/11/2017 11:26:34 AM
Request in Processing
Ros
4/11/2017 11:28:41 AM

Request Sent
Ros
4/11/2017 2:00:59 PM
Awaiting Unfilled Processing
System
4/17/2017 11:24:05 AM
Request in Processing
Ros
4/17/2017 11:24:35 AM
Request Resubmitted for Processing
Ros
4/17/2017 11:24:48 AM
Request Sent

"Awaiting request processing" means: "Your request has been submitted to ILL. ILL staff will review your request for any problems. Requests are processed in the order in which they are received through ILLiad." The definition of "Awaiting Unfilled Processing" is this: "Your request has been sent to potential lending libraries. However, these libraries have been unable to fill your request. ILL is trying to locate additional libraries that may own the material. This process may take several days." In other words, the request was rejected. Three different libraries either never responded, or rejected the request. I confirmed with the librarian that all three of these libraries were of course from the area around Martha's Vineyard, because logically that is where the *Martha's Vineyard Gazette* microfilm would be housed in local institutions in Massachusetts. One could be excused, two is a coincidence, three might be a pattern. It seems suspicious that all three rejected such a mundane request for two roles of film. I wonder how many more rejections I would have received if the Library of Congress had not been the next institution to be asked for the microfilm. I would like to thank Vanessa Mitchell, librarian at the Newspaper & Current Periodical Reading

Room and Government Publications Division, at the Library of Congress for making sure I was able to obtain this microfilm. Without her, we would never have been able to uncover the secret that was contained within, a secret that apparently the editor of the *Gazette* was not alone in trying to keep hidden.

Once obtaining the microfilm I picked it up at the B&ECPL and viewed it at the Grosvenor Room with a second person who wishes to remain anonymous. The parameters above were used to begin the process of finding this second witness. We began looking at the *Gazette* in April 1999 and wrote down the names of all male reporters and continued writing down the names of all male reporters until the September 1999 editions. The process was tedious, but we eventually found what we were looking for. There is a male reporter who began writing for the *Gazette* in late May 1999, and then once September 1999 arrived, his name no longer appeared. It is important to note that this only happens with one male reporter. The other male reporters continue being listed in the newspaper into October. Logically then this must be the student who witnessed the explosion.

In retrospect, I suppose the editor wanted to shield this young man from scrutiny, to protect his life. She probably knew that if she revealed his identity it would be dangerous for him and his family. The attention might be too much for him to be able to handle. The possibility also exists that this person was in high school, and was not a college student. This might account for her not confirming that he was a journalism major. This was probably the prudent decision to make to protect his identity. We have reached the same conclusion as the editor. We will not reveal the name of this man who would probably be in his late 30s by 2017. If anyone is interested in finding out the name for yourself, and confirming what we found, you are welcome to look at the microfilm yourself, and verify this through the same process. My only advice though if you are going to request this film through interlibrary loan, do not bother trying to get it through any libraries in Massachusetts, go directly through the Library of Congress.

When combining the DiNardo interview with the information we found there is no doubt that this person exists, and for now he will remain anonymous. There is really no benefit anyway to publishing his name. Nothing good could come from that, considering how many people have died surrounding the Kennedy assassinations. With that in mind, we should appreciate the courage of witness number three, whose name is widely known, by his own choice to come forward. He was perhaps best positioned to hear Kennedy's plane blown out of the sky. He is the best proof that the Kennedy plane crash was not an accident, but instead an airborne explosion.

## Eyewitness Number Three: Victor Pribanic

The final witness is the only one of the three with which we can attach a name to. He was mentioned, albeit briefly in *The Day John Died* by Christopher Anderson. "The lone fisherman angling for bass off Squibnocket Pond on Martha's Vineyard looked up to see a small aircraft flying toward the Island. Victor Pribanic, a forty-five-year-old Pittsburg attorney who had been coming to the Vineyard for twenty years, thought nothing of it and went back to his fishing. Within moments there was a loud bang..." Also, Anderson mentioned that Pribanic looked out towards the Atlantic to follow the sound of the explosion. This of course is the opposite direction of Falmouth. All three witnesses heard a single bang in the Atlantic, the opposite direction of Falmouth. Squibnocket Pond is on the extreme western end of Martha's Vineyard Island. To look at something going on in Falmouth would be impossible from there. He would have to turn around and look across the entire length of the island. Also, the editor said fireworks were going off in Falmouth, that they were shooting off rockets. Notice the plural for both, in other words more than one "explosion," if that is what you want to label a firework when it goes off. None of the witnesses heard more than one explosion. They did not hear fireworks going off. They heard a single explosion. If fireworks were going off over 30 miles away in Falmouth that is an entirely different event from what these witnesses saw and heard.

This is how the *New York Daily News* reported Pribanic's account in a story on July 21, 1999.

"I heard an explosion over my right shoulder," Pribanic said yesterday in the first interview he has granted since the crash that killed JFK Jr.; his wife, Carolyn Bessette Kennedy, and her sister Lauren Bessette. "It sounded like an explosion. There was no shock wave, but it was a large bang." Pribanic, 45, who has spent his summers on Martha's Vineyard for 20 years, pinpointed the source of the sound about 4 miles offshore, near Nomans Island. He said that just before hearing the noise, he noticed a small aircraft flying low over the water toward the island... Pribanic said he fished until 1 a.m., pulling in one large striper before heading home to bed. When he woke up Saturday morning, he heard the initial reports that Kennedy's plane was missing and felt a sinking feeling in the pit of his stomach. He immediately phoned the Martha's Vineyard Airport. Officials there put him in touch with West Tisbury police, who relayed his information to the National Transportation Safety Board.

Anthony J. Hilder of the Free World Alliance also interviewed Pribanic. Here is a brief explanation of who Hilder is from the Free World Alliance website.

Hilder has been the host of the Millennium 2000 TV series, as well as the popular syndicated radio show Radio Free World. He is the originator of Radio Free America and directly responsible for electing the first independent state Governor of the 20th Century, Wally Hickel of Alaska. While there, he was successful in spearheading the first freedom-of-choice in medicine legislation in the nation. Hilder produced the Illuminati-CFR records narrated by Myron Fagan in 1967. This was the first recorded history of Illuminism in the world. He is the author of *The Warlords of Washington*, done with Curtis B. Dahl...exposing the setup of American involvement in World War II at Pearl Harbor. He has done in excess of 4,400 interviews with politically and culturally significant world figures. He has produced more than 300 successfully-released and highly informative records, audio cassettes and video tapes ranging from *Pawns in the Game* with Commander William Guy Carr to *Red Stars Over Hollywood*...Hilder has been described as "the hardest hitting talk show host in America." He has been thrown off over half-a-dozen major television and radio shows during the broadcast when he ventured into territory forbidden by the mainstream media... He is the author of The Free World Manifesto...Its premise calls for the recognition of all independent linguistic, tribal, racial, ethnic, religious and political nation states as sovereign members of the Free World Alliance.

Pribanic expanded with Hilder on what had been previously reported in the *Daily News*.

Victor Pribanic often goes to Martha's Vineyard to fish for those big striped bass which lay in abundance off the south end of the island. The remnants of the old boardwalk is still there, along with some of the steel poles stuck where the old-timers came from one of the fishing clubs that drew crowds there in the late 1800s. Those places are all closed now, but those who know "the right spot" off Squidnocket Point still take the trip to fish at night in hopes they'll bag some big bass. Vic Pribanic was there fishing the night that JFK Jr.'s airplane was on its approach to the island's overlit airport when the murdered president's only son radioed the control tower at 9:39 p.m. that he was about 10 miles off the island and would drop off his sister-in-law, Lauren Bessette and then take off again between 11 p.m. and 11:30 p.m. for the Hyannis Airport. United Press International, ABC News and WCVB-TV fully confirmed this story. All was well and the sky was moderately clear...All of sudden as a lightning bolt, Pribanic turned abruptly towards the explosion: "I heard a loud impact like a bomb," said Pribanic, a skilled trial lawyer from White Oak, Pennsylvania. At first, he thought it could have been the military, exploding one of their bombs off of No-Man's Island, a small island off the shore. But that couldn't be. It was at night. And they stopped that years ago. Nonetheless, the explosion sounded nearly identical and came seemingly from the sky out over the ocean...What about Victor Pribanic? Is he credible? Yes! I found him to be one of the clearest and most concerned witnesses I've ever come across, as evidenced by his actions after the explosion shattered the calm of his night and changed his life forever. The next day when Pribanic heard the news of the Kennedy crash, he called local aviation officials to tell his story and then eventually wound up talking to Hank Myer of the West Tisbury Police Dept. to tell his story. They went out to the site he fished the night before and he pointed to where the explosion had rocked the night sky. It was in the exact direction where they discovered the plane submerged on the ocean floor many days later. Why didn't the authorities consult with this top witness, ignoring him and spending the better part of the week spending hundreds of thousands of dollars sweeping hundreds of empty square miles for the missing plane? Where Victor Pribanic had pointed as the location of the explosion is exactly where the Coast Guard recovered scattered items from the blown-up plane and near where other debris from the plane had washed ashore. I asked Mr. Pribanic, who returned my call, if he felt that JFK Jr. and his family was murdered. He said, "It's certainly in the realm of possibility."

Considering that Mr. Pribanic's story is so widely known, I concluded that I might have a better chance of getting a reply than with Shepard Smith. I tracked down Pribanic through the website of his law firm located near Pittsburgh, Pennsylvania. Here is a transcript of our email correspondence.

Date: Tuesday, March 7, 2017 at 10:56 AM
To: <vpribanic@pribanic.com>, <vpribanic@gmail.com>
Subject: DO YOU NEED LEGAL HELP? [#201]

Name *
John Koerner
City
Buffalo
State
New York
Email *
jpkoerner@yahoo.com
Tell us about your case. *

This is a personal email for Mr. Pribanic. My name is Professor John Koerner. I teach American History at Erie Community College in Williamsville, N.Y. I apologize for contacting you in this manner. I didn't know what other way I could. I am writing to inquire if you are the same Victor Pribanic who was a witness to the tragic events of July 16, 1999 at Martha's Vineyard. I am doing some research on JFK JR's death and I was wondering if you would be willing to comment further on what you saw. If not, I truly understand and thank you for your time.

Sincerely,
Professor John Koerner

Here was his only reply:

Victor Pribanic <vpribanic@pribanic.com>
To
jpkoerner@yahoo.com
Mar 7 at 6:00 PM
In a trial John – contact me in 2 weeks.

Victor H. Pribanic
PRIBANIC & PRIBANIC
vpribanic@pribanic.com
(412) 672-5444
(412) 672-3715 (fax)

I replied:

John Koerner <jpkoerner@yahoo.com>
To Victor Pribanic
Mar 8 at 11:16 AM
Dear Mr. Pribanic:
Thank you so much for replying. I will contact you in two weeks.
John Koerner

To
Victor Pribanic
Mar 22 at 8:56 AM
Dear Mr. Pribanic: Just wondering if your trial is over and it might be a good time to ask some questions about your experiences in July 1999. Thank you so much for your consideration.

Professor John Koerner
Erie Community College North Campus

I sent the same message a week later. I am disappointed to say that he never replied. It seems unusual that he would not return my messages after his trial was over, even if just to say that he did not want to talk about the plane crash. His reply was so encouraging, especially since he used my first name, gave me a specific time to contact him again, and replied the same day I sent the email. It seems odd that he seemed so willing to discuss his eyewitness testimony at first, and then left three of my emails without even the courtesy of a no comment. Still, I find it impossible to harbor any resentment. He might be tired of talking about this issue, nearly 20 years after it happened, or frightened that too much attention might be harmful to the health of himself, and his family. Whatever the reason, there is still plenty of documented evidence of what he saw in the sky off Martha's Vineyard that tragic night.

Therefore, the weight of the evidence in this case points to this crash as being anything but an accident. There was certainly motive on the part of powerful people and groups to kill John F. Kennedy, Jr., due to his potential threat as a political candidate, and his investigation into the assassination of his father. The official version of this accident as put forward by the NTSB is counterintuitive. As we demonstrated, Kennedy was a skilled, careful pilot who knew how to use autopilot. The weather that night was clear. His call in to air traffic control, exactly one hour into the flight proved he was not suffering from spatial disorientation. He had complete control of the aircraft, also proving his ankle had healed. We also know that the military claimed to have found one of their own downed emergency rescue beacons, and then never revealed anything more about this alleged crash. The simple explanation is that they likely found the Piper Saratoga beacon, and lied about it to allow more time to destroy evidence of a bomb. This of course, would correspond to the eyewitness testimony of three people who either saw or heard an explosion in the sky just before the crash. This indicates that a bomb may have been placed on the plane. We also discussed how the fuel valve was found to be tampered with. The only conclusion any logical person would make then is that this crash was no accident. On July 16, 1999, John Fitzgerald Kennedy, Jr., was assassinated. This realization has tremendous implications. If we could somehow get to the point where enough people in the United States demand a reopening into this investigation, those who murdered John F. Kennedy, Jr., could still be held legally accountable. It is not too late to bring justice in this case, as we near the 20th anniversary in 2019 of that tragic day. My hope is that this book will begin this effort towards justice for both the Kennedy, and the Bessette families.

For a man who was so universally loved and respected by Democrats and Republicans alike for his ability to rise above politics, JFK, Jr., is still missed today in our polarized country. He might have been the kind of president to remind us about the value of service not to yourself, but to the greater good of the country. The hope and promise of President Kennedy's call to service, efforts at racial equality, and struggles for world peace may have lived on in his son, as JFK, Jr., faced the challenges of the strife-filled 21st century. JFK, Jr., was 38 years-old when he died. John F. Kennedy used his brief time in the Congress in the 1950s when he was in his thirties as the beginning of his path to the White House. A brief sojourn in Albany as governor of New York beginning in 2003, even a year, could have put JFK, Jr., on a similar trajectory path to the presidency in 2004. Kennedy would have been 43 years-old on election day that year, the same age that his father was when he took the oath of office on January 20, 1961.

# Works Cited

## Part one – The Motives

http://people.com/celebrity/john-f-kennedy-jr-for-president
-jfks-sons-political-ambition/

https://www.elections.ny.gov/2002ElectionResults.html

http://www.nydailynews.com/archives/news/jfk-jr-mulled-run-
senate-2000-article-1.847866

http://nypost.com/2004/03/16/jfk-jr-mad-at-hill-senate-run-
book/

http://www.nydailynews.com/news/politics/bobby-claims-vic-
tory-keating-article-1.1991856

https://www.nga.org/cms/home/governors/past-governors-bi-
os/page_new_york.html

https://www.whitehouse.gov/1600/presidents/johnfkennedy

https://www.biography.com/people/john-f-kennedy-jr-9542094

https://parade.com/226242/parade/bill-clinton-recalls-where-
he-was-when-he-learned-jfk-died-i-was-heartbroken/

http://articles.chicagotribune.com/1993-07-23/news/93072402
09_1_boys-nation-clinton-and-cohen-jfk

https://www.jfklibrary.org/JFK/The-Kennedy-Family/Jean-Ken-
nedy-Smith.aspx

http://www.nytimes.com/1999/07/24/nyregion/the-kennedy-memorial-the-service-doors-closed-kennedys-offer-their-farewells.html

Leamer, Lawrence, Sons of Camelot: The Fate of An American Dynasty (Harper Collins, New York), 2011

http://www.aparchive.com/metadata/US-John-F-Kennedy-Jr-1988-DNC-Convention-Speech/3d06a60efe2d44b595937f626fcded26

https://www.whitehouse.gov/1600/presidents/johnfkennedy

https://www.biography.com/people/john-f-kennedy-jr-9542094

http://people.com/archive/cover-story-the-sexiest-kennedy-vol-30-no-11/

http://nypost.com/2016/11/03/jfk-jr-predicted-trumps-run-for-president-20-years-ago/

http://people.com/celebrity/john-f-kennedy-jr-for-president-jfks-sons-political-ambition/

http://www.washingtonpost.com/wp-srv/politics/campaigns/wh2000/stories/bush030899.htm

http://www.presidency.ucsb.edu/ws/?pid=77819

McBride, Joseph, Into the Nightmare: My Search for the Killers of President John F. Kennedy and Officer J. D. Tippit (Hightower Press,) 2013

http://www.nytimes.com/1999/07/16/us/bush-forgoes-federal-funds-and-has-no-spending-limit.html

https://www.amazon.com/Into-Nightmare-Killers-President-Kennedy/dp/1939795257

http://www.wnd.com/2013/09/did-george-h-w-bush-witness-jfk-assassination/

http://www.nytimes.com/1988/07/11/us/63-F.B.I.-memo-ties-bush-to-intelligence-agency.html

http://aarclibrary.org/notices/Affidavit_of_George_William_Bush_880921.pdf

http://nsarchive.gwu.edu/coldwar/interviews/episode-11/hilsman1.html

https://www.nytimes.com/2014/03/11/us/politics/roger-hilsman-adviser-to-kennedy-on-vietnam-dies-at-94.html?_r=0

David Halberstam, The Best and the Brightest, (Ballantine Books, New York, 1993)

https://whowhatwhy.org/2013/10/02/bush-and-the-jfk-hit-part-3-where-was-poppy-november-22-1963/

Baker, Russ, Family of Secrets: The Bush Dynasty, America's Invisible Government, and the Hidden History of the Last Fifty Years (Bloomsbury Press, London), 2003

Bryce, Robert, Cronies: Oil, the Bushes, and the Rise of Texas, America's Superstate, (Public Affairs,) 2004.

http://spartacus-educational.com/JFKoildepletion.htm

https://www.jfklibrary.org/Asset-Viewer/Archives/JFKWHA-157.aspx

Nigel Turner, "The Men Who Killed Kennedy," volume 9, BBC

Brown, Madeline Duncan, Texas in the Morning: The Love Story of Madeleine Brown and President Lyndon Baines Johnson (Conservatory Press, New York), 1997.

https://www.youtube.com/results?search_query=saintly+oswald+bush

http://realneo.us/content/jfk-jr-told-world-who-murdered-his-father-%E2%80%93-nobody-was-paying-attention-george-h-w-bush-etc

http://jamesfetzer.blogspot.com/2015/09/did-george-hw-bush-coordinate-jfk-hit.html

https://www.linkedin.com/pulse/order-skull-bones-everything-you-always-wanted-know-were-lamotta-6111332248403918848

http://jfkfacts.org/what-is-the-cia-hiding-about-orlando-bosch/

http://croftsmexico.blogspot.com/2011/05/dark-complected-man-dies.html

Groden, Robert J. The Killing of a President (Penguin Group, New York), 1993, 202-203.

http://jfkfacts.org/top-6-jfk-files-the-cia-still-keeps-secret/

Stich, Rodney, Defrauding America (Silverpeak Enterprises, Inc,), 2005

# Works Cited

https://www.tsl.texas.gov/ref/abouttx/governors.html

https://www.pinterest.com/pin/385480049334034500/

https://www.amazon.com/Dark-Legacy-II-John-Kennedy/dp/B00JRZ0XCY

http://www2.ucsc.edu/whorulesamerica/power/bohemian_grove_spy.html

Domhoff, G. William, The Bohemian Grove and Other Retreats: A Study in Ruling Class Cohesiveness, (McGraw-Hill), 2013.

https://www.google.com/search?q=richard+m+hooke+jfk+-george+bush&tbm=isch&tbo=u&source=univ&sa=X&ved=0a-hUKEwiJ_L3lssDUAhWDHD4KHR5PCeQQ7AkISg&biw=1609&bih=935#imgrc=Gw5jAT7982-0nM:&spf=1497548496610

https://www.biography.com/people/george-w-bush-9232768

Jeffries, Donald, Hidden History: An Expose of Modern Crimes, Conspiracies, and Cover-Ups in American Politics, (Skyhorse Publishing, New York), 2016.

https://www.henrymakow.com/2015/07/JFK-Jr-Death-Was-No-Accident%20.html

http://educationforum.ipbhost.com/index.php?/topic/19322-book-eleven-letters-and-a-poem-john-f-kennedy-jr-to-meg-az-zoni/

http://rense.com/general78/reas.htm

Koerner, John, Why the CIA Killed JFK and Malcolm X: The Secret Drug Trade in Laos, (Chronos Books), 2014.

https://ratical.org/ratville/JFK/USO/appE.html

https://www.jfklibrary.org/JFK/JFK-in-History/Laos.aspx

http://www.history.com/this-day-in-history/marilyn-monroe-is-found-dead

http://bostonreview.net/us/galbraith-exit-strategy-vietnam

http://www.rollingstone.com/culture/features/the-last-confession-of-e-howard-hunt-20070405

Marrs, Jim, Crossfire: The Plot that Killed Kennedy, (Basic Books, revised edition), 2003.

http://www.check-six.com/Crash_Sites/Kennedy-N344S.htm

http://www.bostonmagazine.com/news/blog/2014/06/19/throwback-thursday-ted-kennedys-plane-crashed/

Lewis, Jonathan E., Spy Capitalism: Itek and the C.I.A., (Yale University Press), 2014.

https://books.google.com/books?id=rURdlJJgYcoC&pg=PA295&lpg=PA295&dq=daniel+e+hogan+cia&source=bl&ots=kgVHk-8SO9S&sig=zneoNE0STdQtotOaeZQi1sQlM_4&hl=en&sa=X-&ved=0ahUKEwiZ696XwNDUAhWBGj4KHWGpBVAQ6AEIQ-jAF#v=onepage&q=daniel%20e%20hogan%20cia&f=false

http://www.history.com/this-day-in-history/incident-on-chappaquiddick-island

d'Arc, Joan, and Al Hidell, Conspiracy Reader: From the Deaths of JFK and John Lennon to Government-Sponsored Alien Cover-Ups, "Accident or Ambush," (Skyhorse Publishing), 2012.

https://www.bostonglobe.com/metro/2013/11/24/his-brother-keeper-robert-kennedy-saw-conspiracy-jfk-assassination/TmZ0nfKsB34p69LWUBgsEJ/story.html

http://www.cnn.com/2012/04/28/justice/california-rfk-second-gun/index.html

http://www.dailymail.co.uk/news/article-2066883/Robert-F-Kennedy-assassin-Sirhan-Sirhan-claims-victim-mind-control.html

https://www.youtube.com/watch?v=PekmVRrDs3w

Andersen, Christopher. The Day John Died (Harper Collins, New York), 2001, p. 359.

Obrien, Michael. John F. Kennedy: A Biography (Thomas Dunne Books, New York), 2005.

http://tokinwoman.blogspot.com/2013/11/was-woman-who-smoked-pot-with-jfk.html

https://www.amazon.com/Marys-Mosaic-Conspiracy-Kennedy-Pinchot/dp/1510708928

http://jfkfacts.org/dec-22-1963-truman-calls-for-abolition-of-cia/

http://www.dailymail.co.uk/news/article-2132334/JFKs-mistress-Mary-Pinchot-assassinated-CIA-knew-much.html

http://www.history.com/this-day-in-history/bush-unveils-strategy-for-homeland-security

http://www.nytimes.com/2001/03/16/us/cord-meyer-jr-dies-at-80-communism-fighter-at-cia.html

http://edition.cnn.com/ALLPOLITICS/time/2000/07/31/decided.html

http://www.historycommons.org/context.jsp?item=a071601britishwarning

http://www.historycommons.org/context.jsp?item=a071601bushputinsoul

http://www.cnn.com/2003/ALLPOLITICS/07/16/white.house.tenet/

http://www.presidency.ucsb.edu/ws/index.php?pid=24801

http://www.cnn.com/2005/POLITICS/07/16/bush.radio/

https://georgewbush-whitehouse.archives.gov/news/releases/2007/07/20070716-1.html

http://www.nytimes.com/2008/07/16/washington/16prexy.html

http://politicalticker.blogs.cnn.com/2008/07/16/white-house-refuses-to-release-F.B.I.-reports-in-cia-leak-case/comment-page-1/

http://news.bbc.co.uk/1/hi/world/middle_east/1791564.stm

http://www.globalsecurity.org/intell/world/israel/mossad.htm

Encounters with the Unexplained: "The Kennedy Curse: JFK, Jr.'s, Death – Accident or Assassination?" Grizzly Adams Productions, Inc., February 15, 2002.

http://www.encyclopedia.com/history/asia-and-africa/middle-eastern-history/mossad

https://www.washingtonpost.com/world/national-security/cia-and-mossad-killed-senior-hezbollah-figure-in-car-bombing/2015/01/30/ebb88682-968a-11e4-8005-1924ede3e54a_story.html?utm_term=.44a899f0f6c9

http://www.presstv.com/Detail/2016/05/09/464798/Kennedy-assassination

http://www.veteranstoday.com/2015/06/03/did-israel-assassinate-michael-collins-piper/

## Part Two – The Watered-Down Version Sinks

https://www.ntsb.gov/news/pressreleases/Pages/NTSB_NTSB_releases_final_report_on_investigation_of_crash_of_aircraft_piloted_by_John_F._Kennedy_Jr.aspx

https://www.britannica.com/science/spatial-disorientation

http://www.imdb.com/title/tt0247092/episodes?season=2&ref_=tt_eps_sn_2

Encounters with the Unexplained: "The Kennedy Curse: JFK, Jr.'s, Death – Accident or Assassination?" Grizzly Adams Productions, Inc., February 15, 2002.

https://web.archive.org/web/20130501175552/http://www.ntsb.

gov/aviationquery/brief2.aspx?ev_id=20001212X19354&ntsb-no=NYC99MA178&akey=1

http://www.rense.com/politics5/coverup.htm

https://www.henrymakow.com/2015/07/JFK-Jr-Death-Was-No-Accident%20.html

https://www.youtube.com/watch?v=loPSF9gDDbs

http://www.rense.com/politics5/coverup.htm

https://www.google.com/maps/place/Aquinnah,+MA/@41.5066936,-70.9895644,10.51z/data=!4m5!3m4!1s0x89e53db9c6692fa7:0xd81d9d6e05895611!8m2!3d41.3352369!4d-70.8007864

https://www.youtube.com/watch?v=jfO-JX8LsTc

http://www.nydailynews.com/archives/nydn-features/fly-ing-passion-article-1.840775

https://www.google.com/maps/place/West+Tisbury,+MA/@41.4041015,-70.7295227,12z/data=!3m1!4b1!4m5!3m4!1s0x-89e525140b330571:0x49574e4cfacbc02f!8m2!3d41.3812245!4d-70.6744723

https://www.amazon.com/Kenn-Thomas/e/B000ARC6AK

http://articles.courant.com/1999-07-18/news/9907180016_1_pri-vate-pilots-piper-saratoga-ii-hp-retractable-landing-gear

https://web.archive.org/web/20130501175552/http://www.ntsb.gov/aviationquery/brief2.aspx?ev_id=20001212X19354&ntsb-no=NYC99MA178&akey=1

https://www.faa.gov/regulations_policies/handbooks_manuals/ aircraft/amt_airframe_handbook/media/ama_ch14.pdf

https://usatoday30.usatoday.com/news/index/jfk/jfk087.htm

https://web.archive.org/web/20130501175552/http://www.ntsb. gov/aviationquery/brief2.aspx?ev_id=20001212X19354&ntsb-no=NYC99MA178&akey=1

http://abcnews.go.com/US/story?id=91890&page=1

http://www.nytimes.com/2000/07/07/nyregion/safety-board-blames-pilot-error-in-crash-of-kennedy-plane.html

http://articles.latimes.com/2000/jul/07/news/mn-49042

https://web.archive.org/web/20130501175552/http://www.ntsb. gov/aviationquery/brief2.aspx?ev_id=20001212X19354&ntsb-no=NYC99MA178&akey=1

https://understandingempire.wordpress.com/2-0-a-brief-histo-ry-of-u-s-drones/ (the portion is parenthesis is the author's ad-dition)

Shaw, Ian, G. R. The Predator Empire: Drone Warfare and Full Spectrum Dominance, (University of Minnesota Press, Minneap-olis, Minnesota,) 2016.

Andersen, 347.

http://www.nydailynews.com/archives/news/F.B.I.-suspects-terrorists-trained-small-planes-article-1.921703

http://abcnews.go.com/WNT/story?id=129563&page=1

http://www.cnn.com/ALLPOLITICS/time/1999/07/26/jfk.last.day.html

https://www.intellihub.com/report-15-19-hijackers-911-cia-agents/

http://www.cnn.com/2013/11/12/us/cia-directors-fast-facts/index.html

https://www.washingtonpost.com/news/fact-checker/wp/2016/02/16/bill-clinton-and-the-missed-opportunities-to-kill-osama-bin-laden/?utm_term=.8324f85c1a26

http://www.cnn.com/ALLPOLITICS/stories/1999/07/19/jfkjr.reaction/

http://www.cnn.com/ALLPOLITICS/time/1999/07/26/jfk.last.day.html

http://people.com/celebrity/jfk-jr-sent-bill-clinton-a-surprising-fax-about-monica-lewinsky-controversy/

http://articles.courant.com/1999-07-18/news/9907180016_1_private-pilots-piper-saratoga-ii-hp-retractable-landing-gear

https://groups.google.com/forum/#!topic/alt.politics.usa.congress/XFTBOnbfJ1Q

Encounters with the Unexplained: "The Kennedy Curse: JFK, Jr.'s, Death – Accident or Assassination?" Grizzly Adams Productions, Inc., February 15, 2002.

http://beforeitsnews.com/strange/2015/07/jfk-jr-s-death-was-no-accident-2461200.html

http://www.rense.com/politics4/missingeye.htm

https://www.bing.com/maps?&ty=18&q=Falmouth&vdpid=5488970917415485441&mb=41.56411~-70.627388~41.541302~-70.58889&ppois=41.5523490905762_-70.6174774169922_Falmouth_ ~&cp=41.552349~-70.617477&v=2&sV=1

https://illiad.buffalolib.org/illiad.dll?Action=10&Form=69&Value=139907

https://illiad.buffalolib.org/asset/ILLiad_Status_Definitions.pdf

Anderson, 351.

https://www.google.com/maps/place/Squibnocket+Pond/@41.3363163,-70.77093,13.06z/data=!4m5!3m4!1s0x89e53dc343f-26d75:0x64993a67de13bdb3!8m2!3d41.3201755!4d-70.7852368

http://www.nydailynews.com/archives/news/angler-heard-crash-article-1.846018

http://www.freeworldfilmworks.com/fwa.htm

http://www.netowne.com/conspiracy/konformist/kennedy.htm

## Chronos Books
# HISTORY

Chronos Books is an historical non-fiction imprint. Chronos publishes real history for real people; bringing to life people, places and events in an imaginative, easy-to-digest and accessible way - histories that pass on their stories to a generation of new readers.
If you have enjoyed this book, why not tell other readers by posting a review on your preferred book site. Recent bestsellers from Chronos Books are:

### Lady Katherine Knollys
The Unacknowledged Daughter of King Henry VIII
Sarah-Beth Watkins
A comprehensive account of Katherine Knollys' questionable paternity, her previously unexplored life in the Tudor court and her intriguing relationship with Elizabeth I.
Paperback: 978-1-78279-585-8 ebook: 978-1-78279-584-1

### Cromwell was Framed
Ireland 1649
Tom Reilly
Revealed: The definitive research that proves the Irish nation owes Oliver Cromwell a huge posthumous apology for wrongly convicting him of civilian atrocities in 1649.
Paperback: 978-1-78279-516-2 ebook: 978-1-78279-515-5

## Why The CIA Killed JFK and Malcolm X
The Secret Drug Trade in Laos
John Koerner
A new groundbreaking work presenting evidence that the CIA
silenced JFK to protect its secret drug trade in Laos.
Paperback: 978-1-78279-701-2 ebook: 978-1-78279-700-5

## The Disappearing Ninth Legion
A Popular History
Mark Olly
The Disappearing Ninth Legion examines hard evidence for the
foundation, development, mysterious disappearance, or possi-
ble continuation of Rome's lost Legion.
Paperback: 978-1-84694-559-5 ebook: 978-1-84694-931-9

## Beaten But Not Defeated
Siegfried Moos - A German anti-Nazi who settled in Britain
Merilyn Moos
Siegi Moos, an anti-Nazi and active member of the German
Communist Party, escaped Germany in 1933 and, exiled in
Britain, sought another route to the transformation
of capitalism.
Paperback: 978-1-78279-677-0 ebook: 978-1-78279-676-3

## A Schoolboy's Wartime Letters
An evacuee's life in WWII — A Personal Memoir
Geoffrey Iley
A boy writes home during WWII, revealing his own fascinating
story, full of zest for life, information and humour.
Paperback: 978-1-78279-504-9 ebook: 978-1-78279-503-2

**The Life & Times of the Real Robyn Hoode**
Mark Olly
A journey of discovery. The chronicles of the genuine historical
character, Robyn Hoode, and how he became one of England's
greatest legends.
Paperback: 978-1-78535-059-7 ebook: 978-1-78535-060-3


Readers of ebooks can buy or view any of these bestsellers by
clicking on the live link in the title. Most titles are published in
paperback and as an ebook. Paperbacks are available in
traditional bookshops. Both print and ebook formats are
available online.

Find more titles and sign up to our readers' newsletter at
http://www.johnhuntpublishing.com/history-home

Follow us on Facebook at
https://www.facebook.com/ChronosBooks

and Twitter at https://twitter.com/ChronosBooks